The Testimony of Jesus

The Testimony of Jesus

Vincent A. Orinda

Copyright © 2014 Dr. Vincent A. Orinda

ISBN: 978-9966-1788-1-7

All rights reserved

No part of this publication may be reproduced, distributed, or transmitted in any form or by any means, or stored in any database or retrieval system, without the prior written permission of the author and Sahel Publishing Association.

The author assumes full responsibility for all content of this book

Published by Sahel Publishing Association,
a subsidiary of Sahel Books Inc.
P.O. Box 18007—00100
Nairobi, Kenya
Tel: +011-254-715-596-106
For questions and orders log on to:
www.sahelpublishing.net

A Sahel Book
Nairobi. New Delhi. London. Nashville.

Cover and interior design by Hellen Wahonya Okello
Printed in India

Jesus said this to His disciples: "If anyone would come after me, he must deny himself and take up his cross and follow me" (Mathew 16:24, NIV).

Table of Contents

Prologue.. **11**

One
Jesus the Friend of Job... **17**

Two
The Alpha and the Omega....................................... **30**

Three
The Father and the Son.. **48**

Four
A Child is Born... **77**

Five
Christ Tempted... **96**

Six
The Kingdom of Heaven... **108**

Seven
Christ the Compassionate....................................... **133**

Eight
Come and Drink from the Spring of the Living Water....... **152**

Nine
At the Cross... **173**

Ten
In the Footsteps of Jesus……………….……............... **196**

Eleven
Jesus is Coming Again... **234**

Epilogue................................……………………....…. **259**

PROLOGUE

This book is for all Christians who want to increase in their knowledge of Christ. It is also for non-Christians who want to discover the mystery that is in Christ Jesus. Indeed, it is a book for all who want to find God in their lives and to follow in the footsteps of Jesus. The book relives the story and the testimony of Jesus in a simple and direct manner. The experience I have gone through during the writing of this book has drawn me closer to Christ and I believe my experience will also be the case for all believers who read it. It has given me a deeper meaning of our Savior in my life and I have come to a better understanding of why Christ chose ordinary people, including fishermen and tax collectors, to be His disciples and to do His work.

I have come to understand that Christ can choose to work with an unknowledgeable sinner like myself to do His work. In fact, I have come to understand what Jesus said when He declared that we shall be taught by God (John 6:45). The more I read and learn about Christ, the more I appreciate that I need to be in a closer relationship and daily fellowship with Him. Now, there is no better way to present the truth than to present it as it is. The truth about the Kingdom of Heaven and of the Testimony of Jesus is plainly written in the Bible. The problem is that many of us are shy to read the Bible and even if we do, we do not have the patience and the time to meditate upon the Word. We do not dedicate ourselves to search for the truth as it unfolds in different parts of the Bible and to put the whole story together. If we did this, we would be changed, for the Word of God is powerful. It brings healing and peace to the heart. It brings joy and happiness to the believer and restores those in need. It can initiate the unbeliever to begin searching for the truth.

The Word of God brings fulfillment and contentment in one's life. Above all, the Word leads us to the knowledge of God and of His Son Jesus Christ, who is our Lord and Savior. And when the Word fills our hearts, we would live life and live it abundantly!

This is why we need to focus on the written Word of God to bring to life the Testimony of Jesus in our lives. The question we need to ask ourselves is this: How can we talk about Jesus without knowing the scriptures? For when we search the scriptures, we discover that there is so much to know about Jesus and His merciful work.

In fact, when one thinks he or she knows all about Jesus, one is often surprised to find that there is always something new that emerges as he or she meditates upon the Written Word and as he or she lets the Holy Spirit lead in the study of the Word. In my case, as I went through the writing of this book, I discovered that the more I learnt about Jesus the more I realized I did not know Him. For, to know Him

Prologue

is to follow in His footsteps and do His will to the glory of the Father. It is written that Jesus did so much that if everything He did was to be written, "even the whole world would not have room for the books that would be written" (John 21:25).

I believe we are living in the end of time and that Jesus will soon return to take those whose names are written in the Book of Life home. It is now time for us to know and face the truth about the Kingdom of Heaven and to know about the Testimony of Jesus.

Christ said that the message of the kingdom shall be preached to the ends of the world and then the end will come (Mathew 24:14).

Yes, we shall inherit the Kingdom of Heaven by grace and grace alone. But our first step is to believe and accept Jesus Christ as our Lord and Savior, for it is through Him that we shall inherit the Kingdom. We need to seek the Lord with all our heart and accept our sinfulness. We need to humble ourselves before the Lord as we await the second coming of Jesus. The good news is that God is good. He will forgive us all our sins and soften our stubborn hearts.

As the time of the end draws near, let us pray that the Lord will open our eyes so that we can see the signs of time that are now all around us. As we await the second coming of Christ, we should ask the Lord to protect us from the evil one just as Jesus taught us in the Lord's Prayer. And we should humble ourselves as we follow in the footsteps of Jesus. In our families and in our congregations, let us put self-interest aside and be true servants of the Lord. We should be careful not to be arrogant, bringing divisions among brethren. Those who enjoy divisive engagements should know that they do not know Jesus.

We need to seek the spring of the living water, who is Christ, and carry our cross daily and humbly as we follow Him.

I give thanks to the Lord Almighty for allowing me to be part of the story of Jesus. And I thank my Lord Jesus for giving me the words and directing me in the writing of His Testimony in this book, through the inspiration of the Holy Spirit.

The testimony of Jesus has been told by others and will continue to be told again and again by many more in the future as there is always more to be said about Jesus. This is the everlasting story. I hope that as you read this book, you will gain a greater insight into the secrets of the Kingdom of Heaven as highlighted by Jesus and know more about Him. You will also know about what we should do when each of us decides to take up his or her cross to follow Jesus. There are twelve major issues that those who have decided to carry their cross and deny themselves as they follow Jesus must pay attention to. In a way, these twelve issues have defined what it means for one to carry his or her own cross.

Prologue

Further, the birth of Jesus, His temptation, His ministry that led Him to preach the Kingdom of Heaven and to heal the sick, feed the hungry and raise the dead, and His death and resurrection all come alive in this book. And the love between the Father and the Son and the Father's love for created human beings are well documented.

All the Bible texts used in the book are from the New International Version (1984 and 2011 updated version), except where it is specified. I want to thank all those who have contributed in one way or another in the review and completion of this book.

CHAPTER 1

JESUS THE FRIEND OF JOB

There is perhaps no other book in the Bible where God reveals His inner thoughts about the strengths of any of His children than in the Book of Job. The Lord spoke to Abraham, Moses, Daniel, David, John the Revelator and others in an intimate way. But in the Book of Job, the thoughts of the Lord our God, as He talks directly to the evil one about Job and as He questions Job about who Job thought God was, are graphic and are captured live. God's love, patience and forgiveness of sin are best illustrated in this story of Job.

It is also in the book of Job, where Jesus appears as the Friend of troubled Job, as is described below. Hence, this is perhaps the best place to start as we begin to unpack and to hold on to the Testimony of Jesus. Job was tormented. As he went through his ordeal, he questioned God, wondering why he had to go through such tribulations even when he believed he was faithful to the Lord our God.

Job even demanded that God should take away his life. Job felt he should not have been conceived, and if conceived, he should not have been born. What Job did not know was how highly regarded he was before the Almighty. God's feelings and thoughts about Job are revealed. God talked directly, on a one on one basis and live, with the evil one about Job and made it clear that there was no one on earth like Job for he was a blameless and an upright man who feared God and shunned evil.

But before we go on to read about this conversation between God and Satan, let us take a look at Job's desire in the midst of his tribulations to find a true friend. Job, the man from the land of Uz, said the following in the book of Job chapter 16:

Vs 19: **"Even now my witness is in heaven; my advocate is on high.**
Vs 20: **"My intercessor is my friend as my eyes pour out tears to God;**
Vs 21: **"on behalf of man he pleads with God as one pleads for a friend."**

Yes, a friend indeed. Job needed a true friend as he went through his ordeal. This friend was, is and will forever remain Jesus. Although Job did not know Him then, the Holy Spirit must have revealed to Job that he surely had a Friend who was interceding for him; a friend who took care of each and every situation. The friend of Job, who was there before the creation of the earth and the universe, must have been there with the Father and the Holy Spirit when one day the angels came to present themselves before the Almighty. And guess what, Satan also came with them.

Jesus the Friend of Job

What is amazing is that God did not rebuke Satan or send him away as an unwanted guest. Instead, the Lord just looked at the evil one and simply asked him, "Where have you come from?" Satan answered the Lord saying that he had come "from roaming throughout the earth, going back and forth on it" (Job chapter 1:7). Just imagine the magnitude of this statement: "roaming throughout the earth, going back and forth on it", just like a lion looking for someone to devour. Of course, Satan had been thrown down to the earth after his fall that followed his rebellion in heaven, when he wanted to be like the Most High.

He coveted God's position. His immediate enemy must have been Jesus, who together with the Father and the Holy Spirit formed the Godhead. Satan wanted to be the fourth person in the Godhead but no vacancy had been, and will ever be, advertised. Moreover, no created being could belong to the Triune. Satan knew that he was a created being just as all the angels and man were. But this did not stop him from trying his luck. His proud heart blinded him to the point where he thought he could be like God. As we begin to tell the story of Jesus and of His testimony, the temptations of Job remind us of why Jesus needed to come and rescue us from the craftiness of the evil one, who had fallen from heaven.

It is written in Isaiah Chapter 14:

The Testimony of Jesus

Vs 12: How you have fallen from heaven, morning star, son of the dawn! You have been cast down to earth, you who once laid low the nations!

Vs 13: You said in your heart, "I will ascend to the heavens; I will raise my throne above the stars of God; I will sit enthroned on the mount of assembly, on the utmost heights of Mount Zaphon.

Vs 14: I will ascend above the clouds; I will make myself like the Most High."

And in the book of Ezekiel chapter 28 it is written: Vs12: "...take up a lament concerning the king of Tyre (Satan) and say to him: "This is what the Sovereign Lord says: "You were the seal of perfection, full of wisdom and perfect in beauty.

Vs 13: "You were in Eden, the garden of God; every precious stone adorned you: carnelian, chrysolite, and emerald, topaz, onyx and jasper, lapis lazuli, turquoise and beryl. Your settings and mountings were made of gold; on the day you were created they were prepared.

Vs 14: "You were anointed as a guardian cherub, for so I ordained you. You were on the holy mount of God; you walked among the fiery stones.

Jesus the Friend of Job

Vs 15: "You were blameless in your ways from the day you were created till wickedness was found in you.

Vs 16: "Through your widespread trade you were filled with violence, and you sinned. So I drove you in disgrace from the mount of God and I expelled you, guardian cherub, from the fiery stones.

Vs 17: "Your heart became proud on account of your beauty, and you corrupted your wisdom because of your splendor. So I threw you to the earth; I made a spectacle of you before kings".

So this is the one who came to the party uninvited. He came along with the angels. The loving God decided to engage him in a conversation. And after Satan's answer to God's question about where he had come from, the Lord, who knew what Satan was doing around the earth, said to Satan, "Have you considered my servant Job? There is no one on earth like him; he is blameless and upright, a man who fears God and shuns evil" (Job 1: 8).

This indeed must have been a sobering moment for Satan. In his mind he knew that the Lord had protected Job. He obviously was aware of how blessed Job was. But he decided to challenge God all the same, saying:

Job chapter 1 verse 9: "Does Job fear God for nothing?"

Vs10: "Have you not put a hedge around him and his household and everything he has? You have blessed the work of his hands, so his flocks and herds are spread throughout the land."

Vs 11: "But now stretch out your hand and strike everything he has, and he will surely curse you to your face."

The Lord replied and said to Satan:
Vs 12: "Very well, then, everything he has is in your power, but on the man himself do not lay a finger." Then Satan went out from the presence of the Lord.

The deceiver went out to torment Job. Everything that Job had was taken away. He had seven sons and three daughters; he owned seven thousand sheep, three thousand camels, five hundred yoke of oxen, and five hundred donkeys. It is written that Job was the greatest man among all the people of the East.

The news of Job's losses and calamity came in succession on the same day, but Job was not about to collapse. His response was indeed the most unexpected of any human being. There is no doubt that the response was reminiscent of one who knew and loved his God. He tore up his robe and shaved his head, then fell to the ground to worship the Lord. He said, "Naked I came from my mother's womb, and naked I will depart. The Lord gave and the Lord has taken away; may the name of the Lord be praised" (Job 1:21).

Yes, may the name of the Lord Almighty be praised forever and ever! Satan was very disappointed that the scheme he had hatched did not work out on the first attempt as was the case with Adam and Even in the Garden of Eden.

So the deceiver came a second time and joined the angels again as they presented themselves before the Lord. He came up with a new trick, telling God that "A man will give all he has for his own life" (Job 2:4), and that if Job was affected in his flesh and bones, he would "surely curse the Lord to His face."

So Satan went out and afflicted Job with painful sores from the soles of his feet to the crown of his head. Job noted that his body was full of worms and his skin was broken and festering. The greatest man in the East had fallen. I guess anyone getting near him must have had to bear with the smell that inevitably emanated from his affliction.

No wonder his wife was quick to say, in Job chapter 2 verse 9: "Are you still maintaining your integrity? Curse God and die!" But listen to Job's reply in

verse 10: "You are talking like a foolish woman. Shall we accept good from God, and not trouble?" Job was not ready to listen to bad advice from his companion and he was not going to give up on the Lord.

All this time, Job was not aware of the conversation that had gone on between God and Satan about him. He certainly was not aware that the Lord was watching and was very happy that he would stand the test.

The Lord protected Job's life, which was the greatest treasure Job had. Even after he started questioning God and wondering why he would not die, the Lord kept quiet and was patient with him until the very end of the ordeal. Job's friends made matters worse by tormenting him further with questions and trying to make him loose faith in God.

In all this, Job's heavenly Friend was there beside him. He cared for Job and protected his life. As Job's Friend interceded for Job, there was only one outcome: Job was going to come out of this a winner, destined for glory. Yes, this is the Friend whose testimony this book is all about. Although Job was blameless before God, he also had weaknesses.

First of all, Job saw his children feast during their birthdays, eating and drinking. Somehow, Job was not happy with their feasting and decided to make sacrifices so that they would be purified every time they feasted. As it is written in Job chapter 1 verse 5: "… early in the morning he would sacrifice a burnt offering for each of them, thinking,

Jesus the Friend of Job

"Perhaps my children have sinned and cursed God in their hearts." We are not told what else Job did or could have done to instruct his children against such feasting. Whatever the case, he saw a need to make a sacrifice so as to purify them.

The second weakness Job had was his own admission in Job chapter 3 verse 25 when he said: "What I feared has come upon me; what I dreaded has happened to me." Wow. Job still feared in spite of his faithfulness to God. But just like the Lord through His grace forgives sinners, He had no problems with Job His friend.

The Lord loved Job even when Job was entertaining the unnecessary dialogue with his three rogue friends: Eliphaz the Temanite, Bildad the Shuhite and Zophar the Naamathite. Obviously, this was bad company. Job remained unaware of what God thought about him and his ways. He went to great length to tell God why he thought he should not be suffering as he did.

Let us read together this wonderful testimony and try and weigh or measure ourselves against Job. In a way, Job was asking himself: "Why should I suffer like this yet I have done so much as a God-fearing person?" Let us read Job 31:

Vs 1: I made a covenant with my eyes not to look lustfully at a young woman.

The Testimony of Jesus

Vs 5: If I have walked with falsehood or my foot has hurried after deceit,

Vs 6: let God weigh me in honest scales and he will know I am blameless-

Vs 7: if my steps have turned from the path, if my heart has been led by my eyes, or my hands have been defiled.

Vs 8: then may others eat what I have sown, and may my crops be uprooted.

Vs 9: If my heart has been enticed by a woman, or if I have lurked at my neighbor's door,

Vs 10: then may my wife grind another man's grain, and may other men sleep with her.

Vs 11: For that would have been wicked, a sin to be judged.

Vs 12: It is a fire that burns to destruction; it would have uprooted my harvest.

Vs 13: If I have denied justice to any of my servants, whether male or female, when they had a grievance against me,

Vs: 14 what will I do when God confronts me? What will I answer when called to account?

Vs 15: Did he who made me in the womb make them? Did not the same one form us both within our mothers?

Vs 16: If I have denied the desires of the poor or let the eyes of the widow grow weary,

Vs 17: if I have kept my bread to myself, not sharing it with the fatherless-

Vs 18: but from my youth I reared them as a father would, and from my birth I guided the widow-

Vs 19: if I have seen anyone perishing for lack of clothing, or the needy without garments,

Vs 20: and their hearts did not bless me for warming them with fleece from my sheep,

Vs 21: if I have raised my hand against the fatherless, knowing that I had influence in court,

Vs 22: then let my arm fall from my shoulder, let it be broken off at the joint.

Vs 23: For I dreaded destruction from God, and for fear of His splendor I could not do such things.

Vs 24: If I have put my trust in gold or said to pure gold, "You are my security,"

Vs 25: if I have rejoiced over my great wealth, the fortune my hands had gained,

Vs 26: if I have regarded the sun in its radiance or the moon moving in splendor,

Vs 27: so that my heart was secretly enticed and my hand offered them a kiss of homage,

Vs 28: then these also would be sins to be judged, for I would have been unfaithful to God on high.

    This was vintage Job: God's friend and faithful servant. The 28 verses written above reveal to us just how many sins we commit sometimes without knowing.
    I wonder how many of us can claim to have achieved even half of all the things Job declared in his petition to God. How many? The answer is obvious.
    This is why God has made it clear that salvation cannot be by works, but by grace and grace alone. For if we weighed ourselves against Job's standards, many of us will not see heaven. There is, however, no doubt that if we have faith and let the Lord lead us, we would inevitably avoid many of the above weaknesses and sins in our lives. We would grow from strength to strength as we seek the Lord with all our hearts and with all our minds. Like Job, we would have patience and perseverance.

Jesus the Friend of Job

We would dedicate our lives to serving the Lord as we feed on His Word daily. The story of Job is like the story of salvation. In the end, after God rebuked Him, asking many difficult questions that He could not even begin to answer, the Lord forgave Job and reinstated his health, wealth and gave him children. What a happy ending even for Job's friends who were disobedient to God! The Lord spoke to Eliphaz, one of Job's friends saying: "I am angry with you and your two friends, because you have not spoken the truth about me, as my servant Job has."

The Lord asked them to make available seven bulls for a burnt offering and asked Job to pray for the three friends. The Lord said: "I will accept his (Job's) prayer and not deal with you according to your folly" (Job 42:7-8).

Job interceded for his friends and they were forgiven. As for Job, he was twice blessed. The Lord blessed the latter part of his life more than the former part. And he had seven sons and three daughters, just as he had before his trials. Thus the Lord restored the fortunes of Job.

Similarly, He will also restore us and redeem us through Jesus. The same heavenly Friend Job longed for is our Friend and Savior. Thank you Jesus! We must know and be certain that any trials we go through will, in the end, lead to victory as it happened to Job. But we must remain steadfast and committed to the Lord our God. He has made it possible for our salvation to be assured.

CHAPTER 2

THE ALPHA AND THE OMEGA

"Jesus Christ is the same yesterday, and today and forever."
Hebrews 13:8

It was in the Island of Patmos where John the servant of God came face to face with the Word of God. John experienced the testimony of Jesus Christ. John declared at the outset that those who would read the words of prophesy, contained in the Book of Revelation, are blessed especially if they "take to heart what is written because the time is near" (Revelation 1:3).

The time is near indeed and soon we will see Jesus coming in the clouds with His angels to take us home. But we have been called upon to hold on to the testimony of Jesus even as we await His second coming. John was in Spirit when he heard a loud voice like a trumpet saying: "Write on a scroll what you see and send it to seven churches: To Ephesus, Smyrna, Pergamum, Thyatira, Sardis, Philadelphia and Laodicea" (Revelation 1:11). John says that he turned around to see the voice that was speaking only to see seven golden lampstands and "someone like the Son of Man, dressed in a robe reaching to his feet and with a golden sash around his chest. The hair on his head was white like wool, as white as snow, and his eyes were like

The Alpha and the Omega

blazing fire. His feet were like bronze glowing in a furnace, and his voice was like the sound of rushing waters" (Revelation 1:13-15).

When Jesus appeared to John, His face was like the sun shining in all its brilliance. John fell at the feet of Jesus as though he was dead. But the Savior placed His hand on John and said: "Do not be afraid. I am the First and the Last. I am the Living One; I was dead, and now look, I am alive for ever and ever! And I hold the keys of death and Hades" (Revelation 1:17-18). Jesus had already identified Himself to John saying: "I am the Alpha and the Omega, who is, and who was, and who is to come, the Almighty" (Revelation 1:8). Yes, the Alpha and the Omega spoke loudly and clearly to all.

Jesus is the First and the Last. He was there with the Father before the beginning of time as they created the heavens and the earth and everything therein. And He will be there forever and ever.

As it is written in John chapter 1 verses 1 – 4: "In the beginning was the Word, and the Word was with God, and the Word was God. He was with God in the beginning. Through him all things were made; without him nothing was made that has been made. In him was life, and that life was the light of all men." God placed all things under the feet of Jesus and appointed him to be head over everything (Ephesians 1:22-23).

The Testimony of Jesus

In Christ, we were chosen before creation and predestined for adoption to *sonship* (God's children) through Him. As Apostle Paul said, "In him we have redemption through his blood, the forgiveness of sins, in accordance with riches of God's grace that he lavished on us. With all understanding, he made known to us the mystery of His will according to His good pleasure, which He purposed in Christ, to be put into effect when the times reach their fulfillment–to bring unity to all things in heaven and on earth under Christ" (Ephesians1:7-10).

Jesus is the Word that became flesh and lived among us. He is the true light that gave light to the world. In John chapter 1 verse 10–14, it is written:

Vs 10: "He was in the world, and though the world was made through him, the world did not recognize him."

Vs 11: "He came to that which was his own, but his own did not receive Him."

Vs 12: "Yet to all who did receive him, to those who believed in his name, he gave the right to become children of God."

Vs 14: "The Word became flesh and made his dwelling among us. We have seen his glory, the glory of the one and only Son, who came from the Father, full of grace and

The Alpha and the Omega

truth." This is the testimony of Jesus, which must be told to the whole world. All tongues must confess that Jesus Christ is Lord. God the Father and God the Son are two distinct "persons" who together with the Holy Spirit form the Godhead.

Daniel's vision

In the book of Daniel, the Son of Man was clearly revealed in Daniel's dream. Daniel saw thrones that were set in place and the Ancient of Days (the Father) took His seat. "His clothing was as white as snow; the hair of his head was white like wool. His throne was flaming with fire and its wheels were all ablaze. A river of fire was flowing coming out from before him. Thousands upon thousands attended him; ten thousand times ten thousand stood before him. The court was seated and the books were opened" (Daniel 7:9-10). What a scene!

The Ancient of Days sat on His throne and there was a multitude around Him in a scene that was awesome. It is difficult for one to even begin to imagine the state one would be in if one found himself or herself in the midst of this multitude. I do not know about you, but for me it is not even possible to comprehend how I would be or feel if I were there. My great hope is that you and I will one day be there to see the Ancient of Days and our Lord Jesus Christ as they sit on the throne of God. All I can imagine is that we will worship as never before, singing Holy, Holy, Holy is the Lord Almighty. And we will see what no eye has ever seen and hear what no ear has ever heard.

Let us get back to Daniel's dream and vision. Still in his dream, Daniel says: "In my vision at night I looked, and there before me was one like the Son of Man, coming with the clouds of heaven. He approached the Ancient of Days and was led into His presence. He was given authority, glory and sovereign power; all peoples, nations and men of every language worshipped him. His dominion is an everlasting dominion that will not pass away, and his kingdom is one that will never be destroyed" (Daniel 7:13-14).

Yes, all peoples and all nations should worship Jesus to the glory of the Father who had placed all of them under His (Jesus) feet.

Stephen witnesses the heavenly scene

The revelation of Jesus sitting on the throne with the Father as revealed to Daniel is the same revelation given to John. This is also the same revelation that was given to Stephen who was stoned by his people after he gave a solid testimony about Jesus. Stephen was a man full of God's grace and power (Acts 6:8). He was one of the first faithfuls chosen by the disciples of Jesus to support the ministry of our Lord. He did great wonders and miracles among the people. This did not go well with the members of the synagogue who influenced some men to say that they heard Stephen speak words of blasphemy against Moses and against God.

When Stephen was brought in front of the Sanhedrin to face false accusations, everyone sitting in the Sanhedrin looked intently at him and they saw that his face was like the face of an angel (Acts 6:15).

The high priest in the Sanhedrin asked Stephen whether the charges against him were true. Instead of giving a straight answer, Stephen decided to give a full account of the story of the children of Israel from the time God delivered them from Egypt to the time they rejected Jesus.

Then Stephen turned to those who were about to stone him (Acts 7: 51 – 53) and said: Vs 51: "You stiff-necked people, with uncircumcised hearts and ears! You are just like your fathers: You always resist the Holy Spirit!"

Vs 52: "Was there a prophet your fathers did not persecute? They even killed those who predicted the coming of the Righteous One. And now you have betrayed and murdered Him."

Vs 53: "You have received the law that was put in effect through the angels but have not obeyed it."

When the people in the Sanhedrin heard this, they were annoyed and furious. They were now even more determined to stone Stephen. But before they did this, Stephen looked up to heaven and saw God the Father and Jesus sitting on His right hand. Stephen was full of the Holy Spirit as he looked up to heaven. **"Look,"** he said, **"I see heaven open and the Son of Man standing at the right hand of God"** (Acts 7:55-56). After he said this, he was dragged out of the city and stoned to death. As they were stoning him, Stephen prayed for them saying, "Lord Jesus, receive my spirit." He then fell on his knees and prayed, "Lord, do not hold this sin against them." He died as they stoned him. This sad occasion provided yet another testimony of Jesus, the Son of God, who sits at the right hand of the Father. Jesus, who has been revealed to us, is calling upon us saying, "Here I am! I stand at the door and knock. If anyone hears my voice and opens the door, I will come in and eat with him, and he with me" (Revelation 3:20). He is standing at the door knocking. Yes, Jesus is knocking!

But let us not stop here. Let us find out more about our King and discover more about His testimony in the scriptures. It is overwhelming to realize that all this information is readily available in the Bible yet we have often glossed over it without much thought or attention.

The testimony of Jesus comes alive in the book of Revelation. In his vision, John the servant of God looked up and there before him was a door standing open in heaven. He heard a voice speaking to him saying, "Come up

The Alpha and the Omega

here, and I will show you what must take place after this" (Revelation 4:1). As John looked in through this door, he was in the Spirit and before him was a throne in heaven with someone sitting on it who had an awesome appearance. A rainbow encircled the throne and there were twenty four elders seated on twenty four other thrones. These elders were dressed in white and had crowns of gold on their heads. And from the throne came flashes of light, rumblings and thunder.

John writes that in the centre, around the throne, were four living creatures that were covered with eyes in front and in the back. Day and night, these creatures never stopped saying: "Holy, holy, holy is the Lord Almighty, who was, and is, and is to come" (Revelation 4:8).

What a scene!

John said this about his vision: "Whenever the living creatures give glory, honor and thanks to him who sits on the throne and who lives forever and ever, the twenty four elders fall down before him who sits on the throne, and worship him who lives for ever and ever. They lay their crowns before the throne and say: 'You are worthy, our Lord and God, to receive glory and honor and power, for you created all things, and by your will they were created and have their being'" (Revelation 4:9-11).

John's vision of the Father and the Son was so beautiful. There is no other way of describing it. Hence, we must experience it as it is written, given that this book is about the testimony of Jesus. John said in Revelation chapter 5 verses 1 – 13: Vs 1: Then I saw in the right hand of him who sat on the throne a scroll with writing on both sides and sealed with seven seals.

Vs 2: And I saw a mighty angel proclaiming in a loud voice, "Who is worthy to break the seals and open the scroll?"

Vs 3: But no one in heaven and on earth or under the earth could open the scroll or even look inside it.

Vs 4: I wept and wept because no one was found who was worthy to open the scroll or look inside.

Vs 5: Then one of the elders said to me, "Do not weep! See, the Lion of the tribe of Judah, the Root of David, has triumphed. He is able to open the scroll and its seven seals.

Vs 6: Then I saw a lamb looking as if it had been slain standing at the center of the throne, encircled by the four living creatures and the elders…

Vs 7: He went and took the scroll from the right hand of him who sat on the throne.

Vs 8: And when he had taken it, the four living creatures and the twenty four elders fell down before the lamb. Each one had a harp and they were holding their golden bowls full of incense.

Vs 9: And they sang a new song, saying: "You are worthy to take the scroll and to open its seals, because you were slain, and with your blood you purchased men for God from every tribe and language and people and nation.

Vs 10: "You have made them to be a kingdom and priests to serve our God, and they will reign on the earth."

Vs 11: Then I looked and heard the voice of many angels, numbering thousand upon thousand, and ten thousand times ten thousand. They encircled the throne and the living creatures and the elders.

Vs 12: In a loud voice they sang: "Worthy is the Lamb, who was slain, to receive power and wealth and wisdom and strength and honor and glory and praise!"

Vs 13: Then I heard every creature in heaven and on earth and under the earth and on sea, and all that is in them saying: "To Him who sits on the throne and to the lamb be praise and honor and glory and power forever and ever!" What a scene this was.

It is clear from the above testimony that Jesus is the Lamb, the Son of God who is in oneness with God the

The Testimony of Jesus

Father. The Father Himself testified about Jesus. This is evident in various scriptures in the Bible. One example is when Jesus took with Him three disciples, Peter, James and John, to a mountain. Suddenly Jesus was transfigured and His face shone like the sun and His clothes became white and there with Him stood Moses and Elijah. And while on the mountain, a bright cloud enveloped them and a voice said from the cloud: **"This is my Son, whom I love; with Him I am well pleased. Listen to Him"** (Mathew 17:5). The Father spoke.

One cannot blame Peter who wished that he could build a shelter for the Lord on this mountain. Peter was excited as he witnessed the transfiguration of Jesus and to see Moses and Elijah with Him. So Peter said to Jesus, "Lord, it is good for us to be here. If you wish, I will put up three shelters – one for you, one for Moses and one for Elijah" (Mathew 17:4). Indeed, it was good for Peter, James and John to be there and to be witnesses of this glorious occasion and to hear the Father's testimony about Jesus.

Now, let us turn to Jesus' own testimony during His First coming when He walked the streets of Jerusalem, Nazareth, Judea, Samaria and many other places preaching about the Kingdom of Heaven and the good news about His second return to take us Home.

In the book of John chapter 8, the testimony of Jesus comes alive. Jesus said: "I am the light of the world.

The Alpha and the Omega

Whoever follows me will never walk in darkness, but will have the light of life" (John 8:12). On hearing this, the Pharisees challenged Him saying: "Here you are, appearing as your own witness; your testimony is not valid."

Jesus answered the Pharisees saying: "Even if I testify on my own behalf, my testimony is valid, for I know where I came from and where I am going. You judge by human standards; I pass judgment on no one. But even if I do judge, my decisions are true, because I am not alone. I stand with the Father, who sent me. In your own law it is written that the testimony of two witnesses is true. I am one who testifies for myself; my other witness is the Father, who sent me" (John 8:14-18).

Then the Pharisees asked Jesus: "Where is your Father?" and He answered: "You do not know me or my Father. If you knew me, you would know my Father also" (John 8:19).

Obviously, the Pharisees did not understand what Jesus was saying. What they did not know is that Jesus and the Father are united together with the Holy Spirit in one Godhead. Jesus went on to say: "...When you have lifted up the Son of Man, then you will know that I am he and that I do nothing on my own but speak just what the Father has taught me. The one who sent me is with me; he has not left me alone, for I always do what pleases him" (John 8:28-29).

It is clear from the Scriptures that Jesus is the Son of God, who sits on God's right hand. His testimony must be upheld by all. He is the one who will return to take the elect home and to join the Father as they create a new heaven and a new earth. Jesus said: "Let not your hearts be troubled; you believe in God, believe also in Me. In My Father's house are many mansions; if it were not so, I would have told you. I go to prepare a place for you. And if I go and prepare a place for you, I will come again and receive you to Myself; that where I am, there you may be also" (John 14:1-3, NKJV).

Yes, Christ was there before the beginning and He will be there at the end of this earth as a new heaven and earth will be created where there would be no more sin and God will live among His people. In His own words, He has promised to come again and take us home where we will be with Him and the Father forever and ever.

"Who do you say I am?"

Jesus testified about Himself as the Messiah. And He did this through His word as well as through the many miracles He performed.

On one occasion, He was in Caesarea with His disciples. He asked them: "Who do people say the Son of Man is?" (Mathew 16:13). They replied that some people say Jesus was John the Baptist yet others said He was Elijah and others said He was Jeremiah. Some also thought that He was just another prophet.

The Alpha and the Omega

Then Jesus turned to His disciples and directly asked them: "But what about you? Who do you say I am?" (Mathew 16:15).

This is when Peter said that Jesus was the Messiah, the Son of the living God.

Jesus told Peter: "Blessed are you, Simon son of Jonah, for this was not revealed to you by flesh and blood, but by my Father in heaven" (Mathew 16:17).

And blessed are all who testify as Peter did that Jesus is the Messiah, our Lord and Savior.

"Moses wrote about me"

Christ who was there before the creation of the heavens and the earth was also there when God revealed Himself to mankind through the children of Israel. For there is no doubt that the responsibility placed upon Him by the Father, putting everything under His feet, started long before Jacob's children went to Egypt in search of food and long before they left Egypt for Canaan. And we know that the Father and the Son work in unison and there is also no doubt that the Father is very happy to let Christ do all He does to the Father's glory.

I can imagine that throughout the period God was being revealed to mankind through the children of Israel, Christ was active and was all the time with the Father as the events unfolded.

The Testimony of Jesus

It is therefore not surprising that Jesus said in His own words in the book of John chapter 5 verse 46 that, "Moses wrote about me."

Jesus had been arguing with the leaders in Jerusalem because He was healing people on Sabbath days. He used this opportunity to testify about Himself. Jesus said: "I have a testimony weightier than that of John (The Baptist). For the very work that the Father has given me to finish, and which I am doing, testifies that the Father has sent me. And the Father who sent me has himself testified concerning me" (John 5:36-37).

One of the people Jesus healed on a Sabbath day was an invalid who had been in a pool waiting to jump in when the waters were stirred so that he would get well.

The invalid had waited some thirty eight years to get into the pool but, as he said, no one was ready to help him. Jesus saw his suffering and asked him: "Do you want to get well?" (John 5:6). The invalid did not give a straight answer as he did not even know who was talking to him. All the same, the Lord simply told him to "Get up! Pick up your mat and walk" (John 5:8). The man was cured at once and as he picked up his mat to go, he was confronted by the leaders who told him that it was unlawful for him to carry his mat on a Sabbath day. The leaders ignored the healing wonders of Jesus, but instead complained that the healing of the invalid took place on a Sabbath. They did not know that

The Alpha and the Omega

Jesus was and is the Lord of the Sabbath as Jesus himself testified (Luke 6:5; Mathew 12: 8). Jesus said, "The Sabbath was made for man, not man for the Sabbath. So the Son of Man is Lord even of the Sabbath" (Mark 2:27-28). By this, Jesus must have meant that we are expected to do good to others and bring glory to God every day, including on the Sabbath. He then added, "If any of you has a sheep and it falls into a pit on the Sabbath, will you not take hold of it and lift it out? How much more valuable is a person than sheep! Therefore it is lawful to do good on the Sabbath (Mathew 12:11-12).

Even as Jesus continued to heal the sick and give hope to the lame and the blind each day, including on the Sabbath, the Jewish leaders were not happy and they continued to accuse Him of failing to observe the law.

But Jesus said to them, "My Father is always at work to this very day, and I too am working" (John 5:17). When they heard this, they tried all the more to kill Him. "Not only was He breaking the Sabbath, according them, but He was even calling God His own Father, making himself equal with God" (John 5:18).

Jesus went on to tell them: "I tell you the truth, the Son can do nothing by Himself; He can only do what he sees His Father doing, because whatever the Father does the Son also does. For the Father loves the Son and shows him all he does" (John 5: 19-20).

Jesus told the leaders that He would not accuse them before the Father for their lack of faith in Him. He said: "But do not think I will accuse you before the Father. Your accuser is Moses, on whom your hopes are set. **If you believed Moses, you would believe me, for he wrote about me**. But since you do not believe what he wrote, how are you going to believe what I say?" (John 5: 45-47). Jesus Himself kept the Sabbath and also stated that He had not come to abolish the law but to fulfill it.

In his letter to Corinthians, Paul also wrote about Jesus and the children of Israel as they journeyed towards Canaan. The Apostle Paul wrote thus in the book of 1st Corinthians chapter 10: 1-4: Vs 1: For I do not want you to be ignorant of the fact, brothers and sisters, that our ancestors were all under the cloud and they all passed through the sea.

Vs 2: They were all baptized into Moses in the cloud and in the sea.

Vs 3: They all ate the same spiritual food; vs 4 and drank the same spiritual drink; **they drank from the spiritual rock that accompanied them; and that rock was Christ.**

The Stone the builders rejected

It is written in the Book of Psalms that: "The stone the builders rejected has become the cornerstone" (Psalms 118:22). Jesus related this in a parable saying that He was

The Alpha and the Omega

the stone the builders rejected. This was a parable about a landowner who had planted a vineyard and rented it to some farmers. When the time for harvest came, the landowner sent his servants to collect some fruit but the tenants beat one, killed another and stoned the third. Then the landowner sent more servants to collect the fruit, but the tenants treated them the same way. Finally, the landowner sent his own son, thinking that the tenants would respect the son. However, this time they went too far for they said, "Come let's kill him and take his inheritance" (Mathew 21:38). They then killed the son!

Those who listened to the parable admitted to Jesus that the landowner needed to "bring those wretches to a wretched end" not knowing that they were talking about themselves.

So Jesus said to them: "Have you never read in the Scriptures: 'The stone the builders rejected has become the cornerstone; the Lord has done this and it is marvelous in our eyes?' Therefore I tell you that the kingdom of God will be taken away from you and given to a people who will produce its fruit" (Mathew 21:42).

Jesus is the cornerstone. He is the way and the truth and no one goes to the Father except through Him. He was there in the beginning and He will be there in the end. He is the Alpha and the Omega.

Let us not reject Him.

CHAPTER 3

THE FATHER AND THE SON

If you deny the Son, you deny the Father and if you deny the Father, you deny the Son.

The above are not my words. They came to me in a dream in 1987, when studying in Newcastle, Australia. One night, in a dream, I had a voice saying that: ***"A time is coming and very soon when my church will not know me anymore."*** I was disturbed, but I was not sure what this message was all about.

After a while, still in Newcastle, I heard what I believed was the same voice, in another dream, saying: ***"To deny the Son is to deny the Father and to deny the Father is to deny the Son."*** I felt as if Christ Himself was talking to me. It later dawned on me that the two dreams could be related.

All the same I wondered: Could it be that with time, we would not give glory to the Father as we do to the Son? And, could it be that in fifty or a hundred years to come our children would have little or no knowledge of the Father? Could this be a reversal of where we had come from when people did not know Christ but knew only the Father? Obviously I had no answer for these questions. In the testimony of Jesus, which runs throughout this book, it is

The Father and the Son

clear that the Father, the Son and the Holy Spirit exist in oneness. **There has never been a conflict between them and there will never be one forever and ever.** What one of them does is done for and on behalf of the Triune. This is perfect harmony, where **one plus one plus one is equal to ONE.**

Jesus the Son of God was given authority and responsibility over all creation. He is in-charge. The Father placed everything in His hands and gave Him the seat on His right hand. Yes, Jesus is the Right hand of the Father. Christ is all in all. Everything He does is with and for the Father. At creation He was there, at redemption He took charge then He went back to the Father to continue His work as the intercessor.

Jesus is also the High Priest in the Heavenly Sanctuary and the judge. For Jesus said in the Book of John chapter 5 verses 22-23: *"Moreover, the Father judges no one, but has entrusted all judgment to the Son, that all may honor the Son just as they honor the Father. He who does not honor the Son does not honor the Father, who sent Him."*

Christ did not take upon Himself the honor of being a High Priest in heaven for it is the Father who said to Him: "You are my Son; today I have become your Father." And the Father added: "You are a priest forever, in the order of Melchizedeck" (Hebrew 5:5-6). This is the Christ who will come from Heaven above to take the elect home.

The Testimony of Jesus

The Creator

As it is written, in the beginning was the Word, and the Word (Jesus) was God. He was with God (The Father) in the beginning. Through Him all things were made; without Him nothing was made that has been made (John 1:1-3). Yes, without Christ nothing was made that was made. Similarly, without the Father nothing could have been made that was made. That is why we worship God as our creator and that is the reason the Sabbath was instituted as a day to worship God–one God, the Triune God–as the creator.

Whatever Jesus does is for and with the Father, for they are one in perfect harmony. Jesus is there for us and does everything not for His own glory, but to the glory of the Father. We cannot imagine how things would have turned out without the Godhead. So, as the revelation and the testimony of Jesus continue to unfold, we must be careful not to deny God the Father His place, together with the Son, as our creator. If we do so, we create a nonexistent rift between the Son and the Father. And if we do this, we have also denied the Son for He does everything to the glory of the Father. We have also denied the Father, who is one in all with the Son. In a way, those who find this rift even in creation and fail to credit the Son and the Father in equal measure will in the end **"not know the Son anymore."**

In the book of Genesis God says: "Let us make man in our image, in our likeness" (Genesis 1:26). Notice carefully that the word is "Us" and not "Me." And let us remember the words of Jesus when He said that, "I tell you the truth, the Son can do nothing by Himself; He can only do what he sees His Father doing, because whatever the Father does the Son also does" (John 5:19).

It is written that: "No one has ever seen God, but God the One and Only who is at the Father's side, has made Him known" (John 1:18). We must acknowledge that Christ is God the Son. He is the King and the Lord of the Universe. It is important for us to testify that we are all under Christ to the glory of God the Father.

Yes, we are. Paul adds that: "For He (the Father) has put everything under His (Jesus) feet. Now when it says that "everything" has been put under Him, it is clear that this does not include God himself, who put everything under Christ" (1st Corinthians 15:27).

In the book of Hebrews chapter 1 verses 1-4, it is written: "In the past God spoke to our ancestors through the prophets at many times and in various ways, but in these last days he has spoken to us by his Son, whom he appointed heir of all things, and through whom also he made the universe. The Son is the radiance of God's glory and the exact representation of His being, sustaining all things by his powerful word. After he had provided purification for sins, he sat down at the right hand of the Majesty in heaven. So he became as much superior to the angels as the name he has inherited is superior to theirs." The Lord Almighty, the Ancient of Days, has spoken to us through His Son. This is why, perhaps, the most beautiful verse in the entire Bible is John 3:16: ***"For God so loved the world that He gave His one and only Son, that whoever believes in Him shall not perish but have eternal life."***

This is the love that is beyond human imagination and comprehension. A closer look at this verse reveals at least four major components:

1) The first component of this verse is: "**God loved the world.**" And why not? For what God made did not just happen as the evolutionists would want us to believe. It is unthinkable that the complex things we see could simply evolve. When I look at the colors in birds, the flowers, the butterflies and the beautiful fish under the sea, I try to imagine how these beautiful creatures could have evolved and I am always left speechless. It couldn't have happened! The evolutionists need repentance.

They need to ask God to forgive them for they have been deceived and are misguided. They need to apologize to mankind for telling lies about creation. It would have been better if Darwin used the "Null Hypothesis" that "there is no missing link" in man's life so that if a missing link was found the Null Hypothesis would be rejected. Instead,

The Father and the Son

evolutionists chose to prove the alternative hypothesis that "there is a missing link." Well, they will never find one. God made the earth and populated it with beautiful creatures on land and in the sea. He placed in it the trees, the animals, the birds, the fish and of course man. God looked at what He had created and He declared them "GOOD."

In fact, if scientists went out to prove that "there is no missing link" perhaps by now they would have found that there is really no missing link. So God loved what He had created. He loved the world and the fallen men and women so much that He had to take a drastic step to save what was lost.

2) The second element is: "**He gave His one and only Son.**" This is what it would take to reclaim the lost world and bring back man to God. For Adam and Eve had sinned in the Garden of Eden and God was not about to give up on them – the creatures He made with His hands. The plan of salvation was set in place right from the beginning. Immediately Adam and Eve sinned, God said to the serpent in Genesis 3 verses 14-15: "…Because you have done this, cursed are you above all the livestock and all the wild animals! You will crawl on your belly and you will eat dust all the days of your life and I will put enmity between you and the woman, and between your offspring and hers; he will crush your head and you will strike his feet." This

promise was fulfilled when Christ triumphed over Satan even as His feet and hands were nailed to the Cross. Before this, God had to make a decision as to how the lost mankind would be reclaimed. No one in heaven and in the entire universe could do this restoration job except the one and only Son. This must have been painful. But because of God's love for mankind, Jesus had to come into the world.

3) The third element in John 3:16 is: "**Believe in the Son.**" Jesus gave us this promise: "Let not your hearts be troubled; you believe in God, believe also in Me. In My Father's house are many mansions; if it were not so, I would have told you. I go to prepare a place for you. And if I go and prepare a place for you, I will come again and receive you to Myself; that where I am, there you may be also" (John 14:1-3, NKJV).

Jesus said that He will acknowledge before the Father those who acknowledge Him before others. He declared: "But whoever denies Me before men, him also I will deny before My Father who is in heaven" (Mathew 10:33, NKJV). This is a big challenge for many of us who are often ashamed of Jesus in this sinful world.

We are reluctant to declare our stand before others and many of us are even ashamed to carry the Bible in public. Well, let us know that if we are ashamed of the Lord, He will also be ashamed of us when He comes in His Father's glory. Jesus' promise to those who believe in Him is this: "And whatever you ask in My name, that I will do, that the Father may be glorified in the Son. If you ask anything in My name, I will do it" (John 14:13-14, NKJV).

4) The fourth element in the verse is: **"We will not perish but have eternal life."** This is beautiful. Because of God's love that made Him send His one and only Son, and because of His grace, those who believe in Jesus will come in and eat with Him. The elect who are saved will live with the Lord forever and ever.

Apostle Paul writes this about the second coming of Jesus saying: "Behold, I tell you a mystery: We shall not all sleep, but we shall all be changed – in a moment, in the twinkling of an eye, at the last trumpet. For the trumpet will sound, and the dead will be raised incorruptible, and we shall be changed." (1st Corinthians 15: 51-52, NKJV).

Christ is everything. Without Him the world would be lost and we would all have no hope except to perish when this world comes to an end. But because of the love of the Father, He sent Christ to the world to die for all. Of course, Christ had to face the temptations and he had to submit to the will of the Father.

He glorified the Father in His death, burial and resurrection and went back to heaven to take His position on the right hand of the Father.

The Testimony of Jesus

In the book of Hebrews, it is written: "For to which of the angels did God ever say, "You are my Son; today I have become your Father? Or again, "I will be His Father and He will be my Son?" (Hebrews 1:5). And in verse 13 of the same chapter it is written: "To which of the angels did God ever say, "Sit at my right hand until I make your enemies a footstool for your feet?"

It is only Jesus the Son of Man who can sit on the right Hand of the Father. He is worthy to be praised for He laid the foundations of the earth and the heavens are the work of His hands (Hebrews 1:10).

And this is to the glory of God the Father for whom and with whom Jesus does all things. We know this because Jesus said that the Father and the Son are one and the same and He (Jesus) did everything to the glory of the Father. Jesus said: "Do you not believe that I am in the Father, and the Father is in Me? The words I speak to you I do not speak on My own authority; but the Father who dwells in Me does the works" (John 14:10, NKJV). This is the Father-Son relationship that this chapter is about.

Children of God

The relationship between the Father and Jesus is extended to us as well. For we are also called upon to be in a "sonship" and "daughtership" relationship with the Father and with our Lord Jesus Christ. It is written in the Book of

The Father and the Son

Romans that: "For those who are led by the Spirit of God are children of God. The Spirit you received does not make you slaves, so that you live in fear again, rather, the Spirit you received brought about your adoption to *sonship*. And by Him we cry, 'Abba, Father." The Spirit Himself testifies with our spirit that we are God's children. Now if we are children, then we are heirs – heirs of God and co-heirs with Christ, if indeed we share in His sufferings in order that we also may share in His glory" (Romans 8:14-17). And in Galatians chapter 4:4-5 it is written: "But when the set time had fully come, God sent His Son, born of a woman, born under the law, to redeem those under the law, that we might receive adoption to *sonship*." What a blessed people God's children are!

Further, in Paul's letter to Ephesians, he writes: "Blessed be the God and Father of our Lord Jesus Christ, who has blessed us with every spiritual blessing in the heavenly places in Christ, just as He chose us in Him before the foundation of the world, that we should be holy and without blame before Him in love, having predestined us to adoption as sons by Jesus Christ to Himself, according to the good pleasure on His will, to the praise of the glory of His grace, by which He made us accepted in the Beloved" (Ephesians 1:3-6, NKJV).

The coming of Jesus into the sinful earth was preceded by the birth of John the Baptist, who said this as he

The Testimony of Jesus

ministered and baptized God's children: "I baptize you with water for repentance. But after me comes one who is more powerful than I, whose sandals I am not worthy to carry. He will baptize you with the Holy Spirit and fire" (Mathew 3:11). Jesus went to be baptized by John and as soon as Jesus came out of the water the heavens opened and a voice came from heaven saying: "This is my Son, whom I love; with Him I am well pleased" (Mathew 3:17).

This was yet another testimony by the Father about Jesus. It is, therefore, sobering indeed to know just how blessed we are to be co-heirs with Christ and be called children of the Most High, as it is written in 1st John chapter 3 verse 1: "How great is the love the Father has lavished on us, that we should be called children of God." To be called children of God is beyond words. We must live as God's children knowing that He loves all regardless of whether or not we are righteous or sinners. In any case, we are all sinners and fall short of the glory of God (Romans 3:23). So we should approach God boldly as His beloved children.

And Christ said, "Whatever you ask for in prayer, believe that you have received it, and it will be yours" (Mark 11:24). Jesus brought this message home in the book of Mathew 7 verses 7 and 8: "Ask and it will be given to you; seek and you will find; knock and the door will be opened to you.

For everyone who asks receives; he who seeks finds; and to him who knocks, the door will be opened." He added that if we who are sinners know how to give good gifts to our children, "how much more will your Father in heaven give good gifts to those who ask Him?" (Mathew 7:11).

Among the things the Lord wants us to do as His children is to keep His commandments. This was evident when one day Jesus was tested by a Pharisee, an expert of the law who asked Him the question: "Teacher, which is the greatest commandment in the law?" Jesus answered: "Love the Lord your God with all your heart and with all your soul and with all your mind. This is the first and greatest commandment. And the second is like it: 'Love your neighbor as yourself.' All the Law and the Prophets hang on these two commandments" (Mathew 22: 36-40).

Indeed, all the law rested on these two commandments. Jesus confirmed in this tacit response that the Ten Commandments are all valid.

The first four of the Ten Commandments are summarized in **"Love the Lord your God with all your heart and with all your soul and with all your mind."** For if one loves the Lord in the manner Jesus is saying, then one will:

- Have no other gods before the Lord Almighty (First Commandment).
- Make no idols and will not bow down to any idol (Second Commandment).

- Not misuse the name of the Lord our God (Third Commandment), and
- Remember to keep the Sabbath day by keeping it holy (Fourth Commandment).

Similarly, when Jesus says: **"Love your neighbor as yourself,"** He is reminding us that one must:

- Honor his or her father and mother (Fifth Commandment)
- Not commit murder (Sixth Commandment)
- Not commit adultery (Seventh Commandment)
- Not steal (Eighth Commandment)
- Not give false testimony (Ninth Commandment), and
- Not covet their neighbor's house or wife, or anything that belongs to their neighbor (Tenth Commandment).

Jesus remained obedient to the Father unto death and showed mankind that it is possible to live in obedience to the Lord if we remain in the Lord and if we open the door so that He can come in and live in us. The Lord is saying to us: "My son, do not forget my teaching, but keep my commands in your heart" (Proverbs 3:1). As we have all been put under Jesus by the Father, let us remain obedient

The Father and the Son

to Jesus and through Him remain obedient unto the Father. Among the things Christ did in His relationship with the Father, which we should emulate, are the following:

1) Jesus continually acknowledged the Father, accepting that He does nothing on His own.

Throughout His Mission, Jesus acknowledged the Father and gave glory to Him. Similarly, we who are immediately under Christ must continually acknowledge Him in our lives; giving thanks to the Father through Jesus for the *sonship* experience we have the privilege of enjoying. This is an important step in our relationship with Christ our Friend and Savior.

We must allow Jesus to penetrate our lives right up to the bone marrow. For He says that He is willing and ready to come in and eat with us if only we can open that door. As it is written in Psalm 34 verse 8, let us "taste and see that the Lord is good; blessed is the one who takes refuge in Him."

There is nothing that we can do on our own. In the Book of Isaiah chapter 26:12, it is written: "Lord, you establish peace for us; all that we have accomplished you have done for us." Christ is ready to do everything for us and to carry our burden. For He says: "Come to me, all you who are weary and burdened, and I will give you rest. Take my yoke upon you and learn from me, for I am gentle and humble in heart, and you will find rest for your souls. For my yoke is easy and my burden is light" (Mathew 11:28-30). Let us all accept Christ as our Lord and Savior and lay our burdens at His feet. He will see us through all troubles and strengthen us every time we fall into temptation.

2) Love for the Father

There is no doubt that Jesus showed much love for the Father. As God's children, we are also called upon to love Him and worship Him in spirit and truth. We must love God as David did in his days in a way that was pleasing to the Lord. For it is written that the Lord said this of David: "I have found David son of Jesse a man after my own heart; he will do everything I want him to do" (Acts 12:22).

David is an example to us all. He was tempted and fell into sin, but when he repented the Lord relented and forgave him. This reminds us of what is written: "For the eyes of the Lord range throughout the earth to strengthen those whose hearts are fully committed to Him" (2 Chronicles 16:9). Those who love the Lord must be obedient unto Him just as Christ was obedient unto the Father as He died on the cross. Jesus said, "If you love me, keep my commands" (John 14:15).

Let us not forget that we love the Lord who first loved us. He will take full care of us. That is why Jesus said in these words in Mathew 6:26-30: Vs 26: "Look at the birds of the air; they do not sow or reap or store away in barns, and yet your heavenly Father feeds them. Are you not much more valuable than they?"

Vs 27: "Who of you by worrying can add a single hour to his life?"

Vs 28: "And why do you worry about clothes? See how the flowers of the field grow. They do not labor or spin."

Vs 29: "Yet I tell you that not even Solomon in all his splendor was dressed like one of these."

Vs 30: "If that is how God clothes the grass of the field, which is here today and tomorrow is thrown into fire, will he not much more clothe you – O you of little faith?"

Jesus said that since our heavenly Father knows what we need, we should not worry about what we shall eat, drink or wear because everyone including evil people seek after these things. But one thing we needed to do is to seek the Kingdom of Heaven.

Jesus said: "But seek first the Kingdom of God and His righteousness, and all these things shall be added to you" (Mathew 6:33, NKJV).

Yes, let us first seek the Kingdom of God as our primary duty. Let us show our love and passion to the Father through Christ our Lord and Savior. He is always standing at the door ready to come in. Yes, we must love the Father as Jesus loved Him. And we must love Jesus our Friend and Savior.

3) Christ was humble

To simply say that Christ was humble is an understatement. What Christ did by leaving the throne at the right hand of the Father and coming to a sinful world in a human form to be abused and spat on by created human beings is incomprehensible. I do not know about you, but as for me this is something I find difficult to understand.

How could someone with all the powers in the universe and with all the authority over all creation be as humble as Christ? How? The one who was fully God, yet fully human, could have acted to stop sinful people from touching Him.

But He remained as silent as a Lamb for He had a Mission to fulfill. This was a one-time act. It will never be repeated again. There is no way the Son of God can come again to be tortured and then get crucified by a human being. No way. But this is why the coming of Christ in human form had great meaning to the Father and to the entire universe.

Christ could not be a fair judge unless He tasted for Himself what it was like for fallen human beings to be tempted. Our Lord Jesus Christ allowed Himself to be born, fed on human food, including breast milk, grow up as a

The Father and the Son

child, do carpentry work and be baptized as He embarked on His mission to free the world from sin.

For Christ to accept all the "doubting Thomases," the rebuke by His disciples, especially Peter, the ridicule by members of the Sanhedrin, the walking in hunger and thirst, the witnessing of suffering and death of His people (though He healed many).

Then the carrying of His own cross, on which He was crucified, and finally the separation from the Father for three confounding days, He had to be as lowly as possible and as humble as a lamb. It is written in the book of Isaiah chapter 53:

Vs 5: "But he was pierced for our transgressions, he was crushed for our iniquities; the punishment that brought us peace was on him, and by his wounds we are healed."

Vs 7: "He was oppressed and afflicted, yet he did not open his mouth; He was led like a lamb to the slaughter and as sheep before its shearers is silent, so he did not open His mouth."

This is Jesus Christ our savior. Anyone who thinks that Jesus could just die on the cross the way He did without first deciding to be humble and patient is mistaken. He did not have to die. But because of us, He did. There was no way out. What a blessed people we are! SAVED.

The Testimony of Jesus

Jesus Prayed

Jesus loved to pray. In fact, He was in constant communication with the Father. One day, very early in the morning, Jesus "got up, left the house and went off to a solitary place where he prayed" (Mark 1:35). This was His custom. He would retreat to the mountain or to a solitary place to communicate with the Father.

Just before Christ was arrested to be crucified, He retreated to Mount Olives to pray and His disciples followed Him. Jesus knew that the time to die had come. He prayed to the Father saying: "Father, if you are willing, take this cup from me; yet not my will, but yours be done" (Luke 22:42).

It is written that at this time an angel from heaven appeared to strengthen Him. But He was in such anguish and prayed until His sweat was like drops of blood falling to the ground.

Yes, He sweated blood. He had withdrawn a short distance from His disciples to pray. When He got back to them, He found them asleep and asked them, "Why are you sleeping?" adding, "Get up and pray so that you will not fall into temptation" (Like 22:46). We also must pray continually so that we can better face the temptations that come our way every day.

When Jesus asked His disciples why they were asleep, I believe they did not have a valid reason. Today, many of us are also asleep. So let us ask ourselves this: "Why are we sleeping and not praying enough?" We know the source of everything we need and yet we are reluctant to pray in earnest.

Daniel was a prayer warrior. He is a good example to us. He could not stop praying even when he faced the lion's den. He knew and loved the Lord. Let us take a look at how Daniel talked about the Lord just before he interpreted King Nebuchadnezzar's dream that the king had asked astrologers to tell him about and to interpret.

King Nebuchadnezzar refused to reveal the dream he had and threatened to kill all astrologers if they did not tell him what his dream was. This was obviously an impossible task. But not for the praying Daniel, who praised the God of heaven and said in Daniel chapter 2:

Vs 20: "Praise be to the name of God for ever and ever; wisdom and power are his."

Vs 21: "He changes times and seasons; he sets up kings and deposes them. He gives wisdom to the wise and knowledge to the discerning."

Vs 22: "He reveals deep and hidden things; he knows what lies in darkness, and light dwells in Him." Vs 22: "I thank and praise you, O God of my fathers: You have given me wisdom and power, you have made known to me what we asked you, you have made known to us the dream of the king."

When one listens to what Daniel is saying above, one cannot help but thank God for him. He was indeed close to the Lord and had the fear of the Lord in him. Daniel told King Nebuchadnezzar what the dream was and that he interpreted it by God's grace. Let us also take a look at David, who pleaded with God after he had committed adultery with Bathsheba in what is perhaps one of the most powerful prayers in the Bible. David said in Psalm chapter 51:

Vs 1: "Have mercy on me, O God, according to your unfailing love; blot out my transgressions."

Vs 2: "Wash away all my iniquity and cleanse me from my sin."

Vs 3: "For I know my transgressions, and my sin is always before me."

Vs 4: "Against you, you only, have I sinned and done what is evil in your sight, so that you are proved right when you speak and justified when you judge."

David acknowledged his sins. He was humble and admitted that he was sinful from the time his mother

The Father and the Son

conceived him and asked God to create in him a pure heart and to renew the spirit within him. This is David, a man after God's heart. What more can one say about this prayer that is full of repentance, acknowledgement of the sovereignty of God and willingness to surrender and be contrite. Jesus must have loved to hear Daniel and David pray to the Father. They were straight and did not beat about the bush. They knew their God and the Lord loved them. Christ knew that not everyone could pray like Daniel and David. So He decided to teach us how to pray as it is written in the book of Mathew chapter 6:5-15. Let us read:

Vs 5: "And when you pray, do not be like the hypocrites, for they love to pray standing in the synagogues and on street corners to be seen by others. Truly I tell you, they have received their reward in full."

Vs 6: "But when you pray, go into your room, close the door and pray to your Father, who is unseen. Then your Father, who sees what is done in secret, will reward you."

Vs 7: "And when you pray, do not keep babbling like pagans, for they think they will be heard because of their many words."

Vs 8: "Do not be like them, for your Father knows what you need before you ask Him."

The Testimony of Jesus

Then Jesus gave us the prayer for all times – the Lord's Prayer – in Mathew 6:9-13 as follows:

> "Our Father in heaven, hallowed be your name, your kingdom come, your will be done on earth as it is in heaven. Give us today our daily bread. Forgive us our debts, as we also have forgiven our debtors. And lead us not into temptation, but deliver us from the evil one."

This is the prayer that we must all pray every day. In this prayer we give glory and honor to the Father and we are led to accept God's way in our lives.

Christ knew exactly why He said all that is in this prayer. One underlying factor in the prayer is that we must forgive one another even as we ask our Father to forgive us. Jesus said: "For if you forgive other people when they sin against you, your heavenly Father will also forgive you. But if you do not forgive others their sins, your Father will not forgive your sins" (Mathew 6:14-15).

Jesus is our High Priest, interceding for us even as we offer prayers. In the book of Hebrews it is written: "Therefore, since we have a great High Priest who has ascended into heaven, Jesus the Son of God, let us hold firmly to the faith we profess. For we do not have a High Priest who is unable to empathize with our weaknesses, but we have one who has been tempted in every way, just as we are – yet He did not sin. Let us then approach God's throne of grace with confidence, so that we may receive mercy and find grace to help us in our time of need" (Hebrews 4:14-16).

Prayer is one way of getting close to the Lord. But we should not stop there as most of us do. We keep on asking for more and more every day. Sometimes we fail to recognize when prayers have been answered. We also need to know that when sometimes the Lord says no to our request, it is the correct answer. It is good to go on our knees as we are led by the Spirit.

But this must also be accompanied by faith in God. It must be accompanied by reading or hearing the Word of God. We must read God's Word and meditate upon it daily. We must seek the treasure that is in God's written Word. For this is the bread that we must eat daily to nourish our inner being. Therefore, those who are prayer warriors should also be Bible warriors.

4) Jesus often retreated away from the crowds

On several occasions, Jesus withdrew to a solitary place to be by Himself and sometimes with His disciples to pray and communicate more intensely with the Father. One such incident followed the death of John the Baptist, who was beheaded by King Herod.

It is written that when Jesus heard what had happened, He went "by boat privately to a solitary place" (Mathew

14:13). However, crowds followed Him and they always did. They found Him so that He could not be alone. As usual He did not turn them away.

It is written that "He welcomed them and spoke to them about the Kingdom of God, and healed those who needed healing" (Luke 9:11).

In spite of the nudging by His disciples to send them away because it was getting late in the day, Jesus showed compassion and pity on the crowd and ended up feeding about five thousand men, besides women and children, on five loaves and two fish.

Immediately after He fed the crowds, Jesus made His disciples get into a boat and asked them to go ahead of Him as He went to a mountainside by Himself to pray. He did not want anyone to be around, even His disciples. The disciples heeded and went sailing away in the lake. This happened during the night.

Shortly before dawn, Jesus followed the disciples, walking on water, and when they saw Him they were terrified. He told them: "Take courage! It is I. Don't be afraid" (Mathew 14:27).

The Master had been alone praying. Then He decided to walk on water and once again give a powerful testimony as to who He was. As He climbed into the boat, those who were in the boat worshipped Him saying, "Truly you are the Son of God" (Mathew 14:33).

5) We must also go into the wilderness

As followers of Christ, we also need to retreat from the interference of this world from time to time to dedicate ourselves to God. Just as it was done in the past, Christians should revisit the purpose of **"going into the wilderness"** for a prescribed period. In the days gone, this period was forty days and forty nights. During this period, we should decide on how we want to dedicate ourselves to the Lord.

Christ said that we are in this world but not of the world. He said this as He prayed for His disciples: "My prayer is not that you take them out of the world but to protect them from the evil one. They are not of the world, even as I am not of it" (John 17:15-16).

It is indeed possible to be in the world and yet separate ourselves from it. It is possible to separate from the things around us and go into a form of wilderness wherever we are.

We must spend time at least once a year "to go to the wilderness" for a period of time and be closer to our God and Savior. Here are some of the actions we can take as "we go to a wilderness":

- Decide on the duration you want to be separated from worldly things. Forty days should be the average.
- During this period and beyond, pray continually.

The Testimony of Jesus

- Study and meditate on the Word of God much more than has been the case. Find time in a quiet place to ruminate on God's Word daily.
- Avoid any arguments and idle talk during the declared "wilderness" period.
- Stay in hope and avoid any negative thinking.
- Surrender daily to Christ to the glory of the Father. Simply say, 'Lord I surrender.'
- Forgive everyone – everyday – let the sun not go down before this is done.
- Turn away from anything that does not point to Christ. Keep your eyes firmly focused on Christ.
- Turn away your eyes whenever you are tempted to lust or to covet anything.
- Sing a song unto the Lord.
- Declare a fasting period and decide on the number of days you want to fast. This could be once a week, especially on a Sabbath day, dedicating yourself unto the Lord all day long.
- Keep remembering that we are in this world but not of this world.
- During the wilderness period, do not watch any TV and do not watch news or sports.
- Do not read any newspaper or magazine; just focus on and read the Word of God.

The Father and the Son

- Serve humanity: visit the sick in hospitals, look out for the poor, widows and orphans; give away clothes and food and pray for needy people.
- Eat right – eat mainly vegetables, fruit and nuts.
- Do not drink alcohol.
- Observe physical fitness.
- Interact with nature and every creation around in order to appreciate how great our God is.

As we go into the wilderness, let us remember that with God all things are possible. This is because with Christ in us, it is possible to do all the above and much more. One should set the level of wilderness he or she wants to enter into, and for how long. What is important is that one should try as much as possible to keep to the "wilderness commitments" made.

In concluding this chapter, let us also remember the words written in Colossians 3:1-3: "Since, then, you have been raised with Christ, set your hearts on things above, where Christ is seated at the right hand of God. Set your minds on things above, not on earthly things. **For you died, and your life is now hidden with Christ in God."**

Yes, our lives are hidden with Christ in God. Let us encourage one another in Christ. In the book of Hebrews, it is written: "See to it brothers, that none of you has a sinful, unbelieving heart that turns away from the living God. But encourage one another daily, as long as it is called Today, so

The Testimony of Jesus

that none of you may be hardened by sin's deceitfulness" (Hebrews 3:12-13).

Let us also give glory to our Father in heaven. He is patient and loving and will forgive us all our sins. Let us remember that Jesus is the way to the Father. He says that He is standing at the door, knocking. He wants to come in and eat with us.

Yes, let us open that door. Finally, we must thank God for the Holy Spirit, our counselor, who shows us the way every hour and every minute. We give glory to the Father, the Son and the Holy Spirit in their oneness. And let us declare our love for God by being obedient to Him. Jesus said: "If you love me, keep my commands."

Yes, if we declare that we love God we must open our hearts to Jesus so that He can come in and eat with us. Then, it will be possible for us to be obedient unto the Lord and to keep all His commandments. In achieving this, we will have joy in abundance in our hearts as we continue to search for the Lord and as we hold on to the Testimony of Jesus.

CHAPTER 4

A CHILD IS BORN

"Behold, the virgin shall conceive and bear a Son, and shall call His name Immanuel." (Isaiah 7:14, NKJV)

In the foregoing chapters we have seen who Jesus is and how He is the beloved Son of God the Father. We have seen the Alpha and the Omega sitting on the right hand of the Father.

In this chapter we now see the same Jesus coming into the world to save mankind. Before Adam and Eve fell to the temptation by the evil one, implementation of the plan of salvation commenced. No one else could have been worthy to come in and save mankind except Jesus. He is the only one who could crash the head of the evil one and defeat him.

For God said to the serpent in Genesis 3:15: "And I will put enmity between you and the woman, and between your offspring and hers; he will crush your head and you will strike his feet." Hence the birth of Jesus was no accident. It was a planned event that was also foretold by the prophets. In the book of Zechariah chapter 2 verses 10-11 the Lord declares: "Shout and be glad, O Daughter of Zion. For I am coming, and will live among you. Many nations will be joined with the Lord in that day and will become my people.

The Testimony of Jesus

I (Jesus) will live among you and you will know that the Lord Almighty (the Father) has sent me."

And in the book of Isaiah, it was prophesied: "For to us a child is born, to us a son is given, and the government will be on his shoulders. And he will be called Wonderful Counselor, Mighty God, Everlasting Father, and Prince of Peace" (Isaiah 9:6).

Further, in the book of Micah it is written: "But you, Bethlehem Ephrata, though you are small among the clans of Judah, out of you will come for me one who will be ruler over Israel, whose origins are from old, from ancient times" (Micah 5:2).

It does not end there for in the book of Zechariah it is further written: "Rejoice greatly, Daughter of Zion! Shout, Daughter of Jerusalem! See, your king comes to you, righteous and victorious, lowly and riding on a donkey, on a colt, the foal of a donkey" (Zechariah 9:9). We know that this prophesy was fulfilled as it is written in the book of Mathew 21 verses 1-6, which describe Jesus' triumphal entry into Jerusalem. As Jesus approached Jerusalem, He sent two of His disciples to "Go to the village ahead of you, and at once you will find a donkey tied there, with her colt beside her. Untie them and bring them to me." They did as Jesus instructed. After this, Jesus mounted the donkey and had a triumphal entry into Jerusalem with the crowds shouting "Hosanna to the Son of David!"

A Child is Born

In the book of Jeremiah chapter 33:14-16, it is written:

"'The days are coming' declares the Lord, 'when I will fulfill the good promise I made to the people of Israel and Judah. In those days and at that time I will make a righteous Branch sprout from David's line; he will do what is just and right in the land. In those days Judah will be saved and Jerusalem will live in safety. This is the name by which it will be called: The Lord Our Righteous Savior.'"

Prophet Isaiah capped it all in Isaiah chapter 53 in the following verses: Vs 2: "He grew up before him like a tender shoot, and like a root out of dry ground. He had no beauty or majesty to attract us to him, nothing in his appearance that we should desire him."

Vs 3: "He was despised and rejected by men, a man of sorrows, and familiar with suffering. Like one from whom men hide their faces he was despised, and we esteemed him not."

Vs 4: "Surely he took up our infirmities and carried our sorrows, yet we considered him stricken by God, smitten by him and afflicted."

Vs 5: "But he was pierced for our transgressions, he was crushed for our iniquities; the punishment that brought us peace was on him, by his wounds we are healed."

Vs 6: "We all, like sheep, have gone astray, each of us has turned our own way; and the Lord has laid on him the iniquity of us all."

Vs 7: "He was oppressed and afflicted, yet he did not open his mouth; he was led like a lamb to the slaughter, and as a sheep before her shearers is silent, so he did not open his mouth."

Prophet Isaiah was even more direct when he recorded what the Lord said to Ahaz king of Judah saying: "Hear now, O house of David! Is it a small thing for you to weary men, but will you weary my God also? Therefore the Lord himself will give you a sign: Behold, the virgin shall conceive and bear a Son, and shall call His name Immanuel" (Isaiah 7:13-14, NKJV).

How wonderful and awesome is the Lord our God for He knows the end from the beginning. The evidence presented in the above texts makes it true, as it is written, that the **"Sovereign Lord does nothing without revealing his plan to his servants the prophets"** (Amos 3:7). He told us in advance, through His anointed prophets, that Jesus was to come and save mankind. And Jesus came.

The birth of Jesus

Finally, the time came for Jesus the Messiah to be born to Mary. As it is written, Mary was pledged to be married to

A Child is Born

Joseph, but before they came together, Mary got pregnant even though she was a virgin.

This great occurrence is best written in the book of Luke chapter 1:28-38:

Vs 28: "The angel went to her (Mary) and said: 'Greetings you who are highly favored! The Lord is with you.'" Mary was troubled by the greeting."

Vs 30: "But the angel went on and said to her: 'Do not be afraid, Mary; you have found favor with God.'"

Vs 31: "You will conceive and give birth to a son, and you are to call him Jesus."

Vs 32: "He will be great and will be called the Son of the Most High. The Lord will give him the throne of his father David."

Vs 33: And he will reign over Jacob's descendants forever; his kingdom will never end."

Vs 34: "How will this be," Mary asked the angel, "since I am a virgin?"

Vs 35: "The angel answered, 'The Holy Spirit will come on you, and the power of the Most High will overshadow you. So the holy one to be born will be called the Son of God.'"

Vs 36: "Even Elizabeth your relative is going to have a child in her old age, and she who was said to be unable to conceive is in her sixth month."

Vs 37: "For nothing is impossible with God."

On hearing this, Mary answered in verse 38: "I am the Lord's servant." And Mary added: "May it be to me as you have said." This was fulfillment of God's plan and of all the prophecies about the coming of the Son of Man. With His coming, there were celebrations on earth and in heaven.

The first to celebrate

The first people to celebrate the arrival of our Lord Jesus Christ were Mary, Zechariah the father of John the Baptist, his wife Elizabeth and the unborn John the Baptist. Zechariah was a priest during the reign of Herod king of Judea. Him and his wife Elizabeth, who was a descendant of Aaron, were righteous before God but were childless.

One day, an angel of the Lord appeared to Zechariah and told him: "Do not be afraid, Zechariah; your prayer has been heard. Your wife will bear you a son, and you are to give him the name John" (Luke 1:13).

Zechariah questioned the angel: "How can I be sure of this? I am an old man and my wife is well along in years" (Luke 1:18). When the angel Gabriel heard this, he told Zechariah, "I am Gabriel. I stand in the presence of God,

A Child is Born

and I have been sent to speak to you this good news" (Luke 1:10). But the angel added that Zechariah will not speak again until the promised child was born. And indeed Zechariah became mute as Elizabeth became pregnant.

It was when Elizabeth was six months pregnant that the angel Gabriel appeared to Mary and told her that she would conceive though she was a virgin. After Mary received the news, she decided to visit Elizabeth, her relative. When Elizabeth heard Mary's greeting, the baby in her leaped with joy in the womb. **So the unborn John the Baptist became the first to celebrate the arrival of the Messiah** while still in his mother's womb.

The second person to celebrate the arrival of the Messiah was Elizabeth, the mother of John the Baptist, who said, "But why am I so favored, that the mother of my Lord should come to me? As soon as the sound of your greeting reached my ears, the baby in my womb leaped for joy. Blessed is she who has believed that what the Lord has told her will be accomplished!" (Luke 1:43-45).The third person to celebrate the arrival of the Messiah was Mary herself, who broke into song immediately after the blessed interaction with Elizabeth. Mary sang: "My soul glorifies the Lord and my spirit rejoices in God my Savior, for he has been mindful of the humble servant. From now on, all generations will call me blessed, for the Mighty One has done great things for me – holy is his name" (Luke 1:46-49).

The Testimony of Jesus

The fourth person to celebrate the arrival of the Messiah was Zechariah. Remember that he had been told that he would not speak until his son was born because he had questioned the angel of the Lord who had brought the good news that he would have a son. He said to the angel: "How can I be sure of this? I am an old man and my wife is well on in years" (Luke 1:18).

Now it was eight days after the birth of John when he was to be circumcised as was the custom of the Jewish people. This is the day John's father Zechariah spoke for the first time since John was conceived in his mother's womb. Zechariah could not help but burst into song just as Mary had done. The first words he spoke were praises to the Lord Almighty. He burst into song and was filled with the Holy Spirit as he prophesied saying: "Praise be to the Lord, God of Israel, because he has come to his people and redeemed them. He has raised up a horn of salvation in the house of his servant David (as he said through his holy prophets of long ago" (Luke 1:68-70).

And of John his son he said: "And you, my child, will be called a prophet of the Most High; for you will go before the Lord and prepare the way for him, to give his people the knowledge of salvation through the forgiveness of their sins..." (Luke 1:76-77).

So, the arrival of the Messiah was celebrated before he was born. And I believe there was greater joy in heaven,

A Child is Born

greater than was the case when Mary, Elizabeth, Zechariah and the unborn John the Baptist celebrated joyously with songs and prayers. And of course Joseph also celebrated.

Jesus was born in Bethlehem. It happened that Joseph and Mary travelled from Nazareth, in Galilee, to Bethlehem, where they had to register for a census, which had been ordered by Caesar Augustus. The census was to take place in the entire Roman world. Joseph had to travel to Bethlehem, the town of David, because he belonged to the house and line of David. While they were there, the time came for the Messiah to be born. Mary gave birth to the Savior then wrapped Him in clothes and placed Him in a manger because there was no guestroom available.

The shepherds

After the birth of the Messiah, the shepherds were the first to be told of the good news of the birth of Christ. As it is written in the book of Luke, the Shepherds were in the nearby fields tending their flock when an angel of the Lord appeared to them. This was most symbolic of who Jesus was – a Shepherd. They were the next group of people to celebrate the arrival of the Messiah.

The shepherds were terrified when the angel appeared, but the angel said to them: "Do not be afraid. I bring you good news that will cause great joy for all people. Today in the town of David a savior has been born to you; he is the

Messiah, the Lord. This will be a sign to you: You will find a baby wrapped in cloths and lying in a manger" (Luke 2:8-12). Just as the shepherds were still digesting the news, a great company of heavenly host appeared with the angel, praising God and saying: "Glory to God in the highest heaven, and on earth peace to those on whom his favor rests" (Luke 2:13-14).

As soon as the angels departed from the shepherds, the shepherds went and found Mary, Joseph and the Baby Jesus lying in a manger just as they had been told by the angel. When the shepherds saw Jesus they were overjoyed and they glorified and praised God for all they had heard and seen (Luke 2:16-20).

The Magi

The Magi were the next witnesses to celebrate the birth of Jesus. In the book of Mathew, the history is written of the Magi who went to Jerusalem from the East asking: "Where is the one who has been born king of the Jews? We saw his star when it arose and have come to worship him" (Mathew 2: 1-12).

King Herod heard this and became very disturbed and so were the people of Jerusalem. The king obviously did not want a rival, while at the same time the people of Israel were awaiting a king who would deliver them from the wrath of their enemies.

A Child is Born

So the king inquired from the Magi to tell him the exact time the star had appeared to them and sent them to Bethlehem telling them that if they found the child they should tell him so that he could also "go and worship him." Of course he had other motives as he intended to harm the new born King.

The Magi followed the star they had seen and when it stopped over the place Jesus was born, they went into the house and saw Mary and the child. They bowed down to worship the baby King and presented him with the gifts of gold, frankincense and myrrh. When they completed their mission, they went back to their country avoiding king Herod. After this visit, an angel of the Lord told Joseph in a dream to get up and take baby Jesus to Egypt. So Joseph and Mary took baby Jesus to Egypt even as King Herod gave orders that all boys in Bethlehem aged two years and under should be killed in accordance with the estimated time period he learnt from the Magi. On return from Egypt, after the death of King Herod, Joseph chose to take his family to Galilee where they lived in Nazareth.

Simeon and Anna

Simeon was a righteous and devout man who lived in Jerusalem. The Holy Spirit had revealed to Simeon that he would not die before he saw the Messiah as it is written in Luke 2:25-26. Joseph and Mary who were then living in

The Testimony of Jesus

Nazareth took Jesus to the temple in Jerusalem to present Him to the Lord in accordance with the customs required by their law. This was after Jesus had been circumcised on the eighth day after birth. On this eighth day, before the parents made their trip to Jerusalem, He was named Jesus, the name He had been given before He was born. When Simeon saw Jesus, he took Him in his arms and praised God and said: "Lord, Now You are letting Your servant depart in peace, according to Your word; For my eyes have seen Your salvation which You have prepared before the face of all peoples, a light to bring revelation to the Gentiles and the glory of Your people Israel" (Luke 2:29-32, NKJV). At this same time, there was a prophetess, Anna, who was at the temple for it is written that she never left the temple but worshiped night and day, fasting and praying (Luke 2:37-38). She came to them and gave thanks to God and spoke about Jesus to all who were looking forward to the redemption of Jerusalem.

This is the story of the birth of Jesus. I want to examine a number of key elements in this dramatic entry of the Lord our Savior into the lost world.

- First, it is "the good news that causes great joy for all people" as stated by the angel who broke the good news of the arrival of Christ to the shepherds. Yes, the birth of Jesus was, and will remain, a great

A Child is Born

joy to the entire universe as it heralded hope for the lost world.

- The second element of this wonderful event is that celebrations broke out on earth and in heaven as soon as the Son of Man was conceived in Virgin Mary's womb. When the angel Gabriel told Mary that she was going to be with a child she asked: "How will this be, since I am a virgin?" But the angel Gabriel reassured her saying that "Even Elizabeth your relative is going to have a child in her old age, and she who was said to be unable to conceive is in her sixth month. For nothing is impossible with God" (Luke 1:36-37). I can imagine that the Father was keeping a close eye on everything. This was a point of no return. The Mission to save the lost could not be aborted. All systems were set to go. I can also imagine that the angels circled the Throne of Mercy with joy, praising the Father and cheering the Son as He embarked on His Mission. There was joy in heaven. Also, as the angel of the Lord broke the news to the shepherds after the birth of Jesus, suddenly a great company of heavenly hosts appeared with the angels, praising God and saying: "Glory to God in the highest heaven, and on earth peace to men on whom his favor rests" (Luke 2:14).

The Testimony of Jesus

- The third element is that Jesus came into the world as a humble Shepherd who was born in a manger. Yes, a King born in a manger! This was surprising. But perhaps what was not surprising is that the first people outside the immediate family to see Him were shepherds, who were in a nearby field. This indeed was symbolic, for it was not just by chance that the shepherds were there at this particular time and that the heavenly hosts appeared and celebrated with them. Yes, a Shepherd was born and was welcomed by fellow shepherds in the presence of the angels. Jesus the good Shepherd was born.
- The fourth element was the order and the form of celebrations which began immediately the Mission started. And as we have seen, the first to celebrate the arrival of the Messiah was the unborn John the Baptist, who leaped with joy in his mother's womb. John was to prepare the way for Jesus. And this started when both of them were in their mothers' wombs. The unborn John, who leaped with joy, was only six months old in his mother's womb. Elizabeth followed with praises to the Almighty, then Mary and Zechariah followed with songs and praises.
- The fifth element is that the coming of Christ into the world over 2000 years ago brought joy and hope

A Child is Born

to the world. It also brought redemption and salvation to mankind. The atonement of our sins at the cross was the end result of this Mission. There would be no need for any more sacrifices for sin as Christ took away every sin as He died on the Cross. All the earthly sacrifices were no longer necessary.

The time to save the world had arrived. And Jesus told His disciples that they were blessed to see Him. He said: "Blessed are the eyes that see what you see. For I tell you that many prophets and kings wanted to see what you see but did not see it, and to hear what you hear but did not hear it" (Luke 10:23-24).

Christmas

Today, the whole world continues to celebrate the birth of Jesus as we await His second coming. But all Christians need to know that the way the birth of Christ was celebrated at the beginning as described above is not the same as it is being done today.

How wonderful it would be if we celebrated the birth of our Savior as was originally done after His birth. The celebrations centred on giving glory to the Almighty and singing songs of praise unto Him. The Magi gave gifts but this was to the Son. Our gifts should be centered on giving glory to God. We should remember the poor, the orphans, the widows and the sick amongst us. We do not give glory

The Testimony of Jesus

to Christ if we simply focus on Christmas presents to ourselves and our families and none to Him.

I would like to suggest that all Christians should give serious consideration to Christ-like celebration of the birth of the Messiah. As we celebrate the birth of Jesus, let us remember His words when He said: "For I was hungry and you gave me nothing to eat, I was thirsty and you gave me nothing to drink. I was a stranger and you did not invite me in, I needed clothes and you did not clothe me, I was sick and in prison and you did not look after me" (Mathew 25:42-43).

It is clear what Jesus is telling us: We need to help the needy even as we wait for His second coming. But what do most people do as they celebrate Christmas? In addition to buying gifts to family members and to friends, Christmas has become a period for merrymaking and drunkenness.

Let us remember that we will glorify God if we centered our celebrations on the reason Jesus came into the world in the first place. He came to save the lost and to reunite us with the Father.

The main message Jesus left with us was: "Repent, for the Kingdom of Heaven is near." And He also told us to go and make disciples of all nations. So why don't we focus on spreading the message of the Kingdom as we await the second coming of Christ? Would it not be wonderful if the celebration of the birth of Christ focused on bringing

A Child is Born

people closer to Him instead of the intense focus on earthly pleasures?

Origins of Christmas

Let us now take a brief look at the origins of Christmas. It is apparent that we have all grown to accept certain traditions as part of the celebration of Christmas without paying much attention as to where they came from. The birth of Christ was hijacked many years ago and became an opportunity to incorporate pagan practices many of which had little meaning for Christians.

First of all, it is very clear that no one really knows the exact date when Jesus was born. Yes, it may seem logical that a day needed to be found to celebrate the birth of our Savior. However, it is common knowledge that the exact date of the birth of Jesus is not known to us. All the same, 25th December was chosen by those who wanted to bring paganism into Christianity.

In *Wikipedia*, it is written that *Dies Natalis Solis Invicti*, which means "the birthday of the Unconquered Sun," was observed on 25th December as inaugurated by the Roman Emperor Aurelian to celebrate the sun god. Roman pagans observed the holiday of Saturnalia, a week long period of lawlessness, celebrated between 17th to 25th December each year. It was during the reign of the emperor Constantine that this celebration was assimilated as the celebration of the

A Child is Born

birthday of Jesus, associating this with the 'sun of righteousness' mentioned in the book of Malachi 4:2. Further, there were other considerations at the time to justify the designation of December 25 as Christmas day. These include estimation of the date when Christ was born. I invite you to Google the 'history of Christmas' to find out more.

Other practices during Christmas celebrations such as the Christmas tree, the giving of gifts and Santa Clause (Father Christmas) are all associated with non-Christian practices. Pagans had, for example, worshipped trees in the forest or brought them into their homes and decorated them. In fact, in the 19th Century, during the Protestant Reformation, there were groups such as the Puritans, which strongly condemned the celebration of Christmas. In England, the Puritan rulers banned Christmas in 1647 and it was not until 1660 when the celebrations were restored by King Charles II. Similarly the Puritans of New England in the then Colonial America strongly disapproved of Christmas and the celebrations were outlawed in Boston from 1659 to 1681.

But today, all the concerns the early Christians had about the way the birth of Christ was being celebrated have all been forgotten. However, I believe that there are Christians who truly celebrate the birth of the Messiah in a manner that glorifies the Lord. But at the same time, there are many

A Child is Born

who just celebrate Christmas without knowing what they are celebrating. Whatever the case, Christmas is with us. However, in these last days, we need to look back and ask ourselves the question: "How should we celebrate the birth of the Savior?" Whatever is the answer, one thing is clear, we need to change and focus on Christ and on service to the less fortunate.

As I conclude this chapter, I am left speechless as I imagine the magnitude of the event of the birth of our Savior and redeemer. It was prophesied and it occurred. Now the Second Coming has been spoken of by Christ Himself and it is coming. And this time, He will come in His full glory.

CHAPTER 5

CHRIST TEMPTED

The temptation of Jesus is among the major events during His Mission to rescue mankind and to save the world. It cannot be that Christ got tempted without a prior knowledge in the heavenly realms that this would happen. We know from the onset that there would be a struggle between Jesus and the evil one as was first pronounced in Genesis 3:15 when God said to the serpent: "And I will put enmity between you and the woman, and between your offspring and hers; he will crush your head and you will strike his feet."

In this chapter, let us take a look at the significance of the temptation of Jesus and its relevance for us today. The deceiver was at work soon after he was thrown down to earth and is still very much at work today.

The evil one succeeded when he tempted Adam and Eve and remained successful many times when he tempted mankind thereafter.

Today, he remains successful in luring away many souls from Christ. The approach applied by the deceiver is often surprisingly very simple. With Adam and Eve, he used a basic necessity–food. And with Job, he attacked Job's children, his property and his health.

Christ Tempted

Now with Jesus, the evil one must have given a very careful and serious consideration as to the kind of temptation he would apply. He must have made a selection of what he thought were the best set of questions he would put to Jesus, given that the evil one knew exactly who he was dealing with.

Even as the deceiver plotted how to attack the Son of Man, I want to imagine that the Father was sitting pretty on His throne, knowing fully well that in the end His One and Only Son would triumph. The entire heaven was watching as the Son of Man went into battle. It was a "now or never" event. Then the moment came and the battle began. Jesus was first led by the Spirit to the desert, where He fasted for forty days and forty nights. He was hungry but ready for the spiritual war. Ready. If Christ failed the test then everything would have been finished in a flash. I want to imagine that if the devil had succeeded in any of the three temptations he put to Jesus, orders would have been given to finish the evil one straight away and the world would have come to an immediate end.

But wait.

Jesus still had work to do to save mankind. So there was no chance that the Mission would fail. No chance.

The battle started. The first to throw the punch was the evil one. He said: "If you are the Son of God, tell these stones to become bread" (Mathew 4:3). This must have looked like a very easy task for the Son of God for He had power to do greater things than this.

The heavenly host, with the Father sitting on the throne watching and the angels cheering, was ready to witness this final round of the controversy between Christ and the evil one which started in heaven and resulted in Satan being thrown down to earth. Christ had won the Heavenly Round. Now it was time for the two to settle matters, once and for all, right here on planet earth.

Satan had to use his strongest weapon. So he remembered that the "Food Thing" had worked for him before as he tempted Adam and Eve in the Garden of Eden. And somehow, he was convinced that it would work again with Jesus.

When the serpent approached Eve, he said: "Did God really say, 'You must not eat from any tree in the garden'?" Eve knew exactly what the Lord had commanded and answered: "We may eat from the trees in the Garden, but God did say, 'You must not eat from the tree that is in the middle of the garden, and you must not touch it, or you die.'" But the serpent was quick to reply to Eve: "You will not surely die," adding, "For God knows that when you eat of it your eyes will be opened and you will be like God, knowing good and evil." Eve looked at the tree and saw that its fruit was **"good for food"** and **"pleasing to the eye"** and also **"desirable for wisdom."** Eve made two big

Christ Tempted

mistakes: Firstly, she started to "reason" with the devil and secondly, she took a second look at the tree and the fruit. She then took some of the fruit ate it and also gave some to her husband Adam. That is the moment Satan declared: "I got you." Adam and Eve were deceived (Genesis 3:1-6).

The "Food Thing" was also used when Esau sold his birthright to his brother Jacob. One day Esau found Jacob making some stew and told him, "Quick, let me have some of that red stew! I'm finished!" Jacob responded and said, "First sell me your birthright." So Esau who must have been very hungry and thought he would die said, "What good is my birthright to me?" He wanted the food.

So Jacob made him swear before giving him some stew. And as Esau ate the food, he sold his birthright (Genesis 25:29-34). Well, the evil one was not about to get Jesus on the "Food Thing." Notice that after Satan threw the first punch, Jesus did not engage him in any dialogue.

Remember, that the task Satan was telling Jesus to do was not difficult for Him. He could have commanded the stones and they could become food instantly. And the food would have been hot and delicious. Jesus was very hungry after 40 days and nights of fasting so He could do with some good food. Satan had made his calculations and was sure of a positive outcome. Instead, Jesus went straight into the scriptures and immediately said: "It is written: 'Man shall not live on bread alone, but on every word that comes from the mouth of God'" (Mathew 4:4). The Mission was on and there was no time for food. Satan had no further line of questioning on the "Food Thing" and moved on to the next temptation. I want to imagine that it was now Jesus' turn to say: "I got you."

Round one of the contest was completed. If there was a referee, he could have given Jesus a score of 10 out of 10 and the devil would have scored zero. Let us stop for a moment to look at what happened here.

First, the temptation focused on food. And Christ was tempted when He was in His real point of need. Today, I believe, Satan still uses this line of temptation on mankind – an approach that is simple, pointed, disguised and applied at the point of one's need. This is the **Food Approach**. Satan is using this "food thing" on mankind even today as many bad deeps are centred around "eating." He knows that we hunger and thirst for earthly things and are easily swayed into sinful actions because of them.

Secondly, let us see how Jesus responded: No dialogue with the evil one, no emotion. He simply went to the scriptures. He must have known that this is what Satan hates most. Anyone turning to the word of God pierces the heart of the evil one with the sharpest arrow. So Christ pulled the trigger and the outcome was certain. This is a lesson for all of us today: We should never reason with the evil one nor with evil-minded people and we should not

Christ Tempted

take a second look at whatever our temptations are focused on as was the case with Adam and Eve.

Thirdly, we notice that once defeated, the evil one wasted no time. He went straight to the next temptation. And this should be another lesson for us: When we think we have triumphed, we must not sit back and feel that we have conquered. Instead, we must be humble, pray more and ruminate on the word of God daily. We must stay focused on Jesus.

The three opening words by Christ–"IT IS WRITTEN" –must ring in our ears all the time. But here comes the challenge: We cannot have knowledge of scriptures unless we choose to love the Lord and to meditate upon His word daily.

Listen to the Lord's plea to the children of Israel through Moses soon after the Ten Commandments were given to them.

The Lord said: "Love the Lord your God with all your heart and with all your soul and with all your strength. These commandments I give you today are to be upon your hearts. Impress them on your children. Talk about them when you sit at home and when you walk along the road, when you sit down and when you get up. Tie them as symbols on your hands and bind them on your foreheads. Write them on the doorframes of your houses and on your gates" (Deuteronomy 6:5-9).

Yes, this is what it takes. For at the time of temptation, there is no chance or opportunity for one to look for the Bible and search for relevant quotes in the scriptures. In this struggle, let us remember the words of Paul in his letter to the Philippians. He was talking about the righteousness that comes from God by faith when he said: Vs 12: "Not that I have already attained, or am already perfected; but I press on, that I may lay hold of that for which Christ Jesus has also laid hold of me." Paul added in Vs 13: "Brethren, I do not count myself to have apprehended; but one thing I do, forgetting those things which are behind and reaching forward to those things which are ahead." Vs 14: "I press towards the goal for the prize of the upward call of God in Christ Jesus" (Philippians 3:12-14, NKJV).

We need to be watchful and not sit back and feel that we are righteous and "have made it" in our search for salvation. This is because the strong will also face tough challenges and will continue to have many temptations. Therefore, as Paul says, we need to press on and keep our eyes firmly focused on the prize that awaits us at the second coming of our Lord and Savior.

The Second Temptation
After the first temptation failed, Jesus was taken to the highest point of the temple in the holy city and the devil said to Him: "If you are the Son of God, throw yourself

Christ Tempted

down. For it is written: 'He will command his angels concerning you, and they will lift you up in their hands, so that you will not strike your foot against a stone.'" Jesus did not enter into a dialogue with the devil. He simply answered: "It is written: 'Do not put the Lord your God to the test'" (Mathew 4:5-6). Notice how the evil one introduces the temptation as he said, "If you are the Son of God." Of course the evil one knew very well that Jesus was the Son of God. So why ask this question? I believe that the evil one was trying too hard and may be thought that Jesus would be upset with this insulting approach. But the Lord stayed focused on the battle.

The devil also knew that the Father was watching and that all the angles were cheering Jesus on since heaven must have been on high alert as this event was unfolding. No one had ever tested Jesus before in this manner. No one has the audacity to put a doubt as to whether or not Jesus was the Son of God. Well, the evil one did. Obviously, if Adam and Eve had not sinned, this event would not have taken place. But the Mission was on so everything was to take place as planned.

Notice also that the devil referred to the written word when he said: "you will not strike your foot against a stone." He certainly remembered God's warning to him in Genesis 3:15 when God said: "And I will put enmity between you and the woman, and between your offspring and hers; he

The Testimony of Jesus

will crush your head and you will strike his feet." Jesus was already "crushing the head of Satan" but the time had not yet come for the nailing of His feet on the cross.

Satan also knew that Jesus was fully God and fully human. As a God, even if He fell, Jesus would not harm Himself except that He would have done so at the command of the evil one. This could not happen. Satan also knew that if Jesus fell in His human form, His bones would be broken and perhaps he could even die before the Mission was accomplished. But again this was not going to happen.

Well, there is no doubt that the evil one is crafty. Today he still uses this method just as he uses the "Food Thing." Many times we convince ourselves that "God will forgive us anyway" if we fell into sin. We say to ourselves: "Once saved, always saved." And many times we sin knowingly yet we do so believing that God will forgive us from such fall when we pray. Today many of us have become complacent and are happy to simply carry our Bibles to places of worship, not caring to fully surrender our lives to Christ. We believe that as members of a given religion, we have the assurance of salvation and see no need to seek the Lord our God with all our hearts and minds. The good news is that in all this, we have a friend. Yes, the Lord is merciful and through His Grace He will always forgive us. But as Jesus told Satan, we should not put the Lord our God to the test.

One day we will have done one more intentional sin that leads us to eternal death: The unforgivable sin of disobedience against the Holy Spirit. We will have fallen from a height and there may be no angels to hold us and rescue us from the fall.

The Third Temptation
In the third temptation, it is written that the devil took Jesus to a very high mountain and showed Him all the kingdoms of the world and their splendor. The devil told Jesus that: "All this I will give you, if you will bow down and worship me." And again the Master replied: "Away from me, Satan! For it is written: Worship the Lord your God and serve Him only" (Mathew 4:10). When the devil heard this, he left Jesus and the angels came and attended Him (Mathew 4:11). He must have gone away from Jesus with the words "IT IS WRITTEN" ringing loudly in his ears to his anguish.

Once again Christ must have said: "Got you!" And this was Mission accomplished. But the third temptation is very common to us today. The evil one is busy showing us an earthly kingdom and what it has to offer. We are quick to look for riches and prosperity at all cost. We are busy worshipping money and bowing down to earthly gods, including celebrities and sports heroes. The evil one has blinded our eyes and we do not see these things we bow to as gods. We have been deceived!

The Testimony of Jesus

In these three temptations, it has been proven beyond any doubt that with God, the fallen man could stand the temptations from the deceiver. Now what remained was for Jesus to die on the cross and atone for our sins. If this first part of His Mission had failed, then there would have been no Cross. But, of course, the failure of the Mission was not an option.

Today, the evil one is using the three temptations he applied in his battle with Jesus. It is evident that men and women have come to love the world and what it offers. People are longing for pleasures of the world and its splendor. Today **the evil one has taken us on a hill** and is showing us the pleasures and riches of the world.

There are many people who are ready to do anything to get these riches. And there are many self-declared prophets who are preaching prosperity and great rewards to those who pay large sums of money and offer other gifts so as to gain much wealth. They call it "planting a seed." These self-declared prophets have forgotten their primary role of preaching the gospel of the Kingdom of Heaven and eternal life. Instead, they preach good life and prosperity here on earth.

There is nothing wrong with prosperity on earth. Abraham and Job were very prosperous people. However, Abraham and Job were driven by their deep love for God. Even when Job lost everything he remained steadfast in his

Christ Tempted

love for the Lord. What is not right is the determination by many today to ignore the message of the Kingdom of Heaven and instead they focus on earthly pleasures and riches. And those who gain prosperity do not use their acquisitions to serve God and to provide for the less fortunate.

In the book of Galatians it is written: "A man who sows to please his sinful nature will reap destruction; the one who sows to please the Spirit, from the Spirit will reap eternal life" (Galatians 6:8).

Let us pray that the Lord will strengthen us as we journey in this sinful world. And let us open the doors of our hearts for Christ to come in and eat with us. He was tempted and He understands our situation (Hebrews 4:15). Therefore, with Him in us, all things are possible.

CHAPTER 6

THE KINGDOM OF HEAVEN

"But seek first His kingdom and His righteousness, and all these things will be given to you as well." (Mathew 6:33)

Jesus came out of the desert after His temptation and went to Galilee, where He lived in a town called Nazareth. He had received the news that John the Baptist was arrested. John's work was done and the Master he preceded was ready to start His work. Jesus left Nazareth and went to live in Capernaum. From that time, He began to preach saying: **"Repent, for the Kingdom of Heaven is near"** (Mathew 4:17).

Thus, the Mission Christ embarked on to reclaim the lost world and its people to once again be in harmony with, and part of, the Kingdom of Heaven continued. This harmony that existed from creation had been broken in the Garden of Eden. It is not surprising, therefore, that the first words Jesus uttered as soon as He defeated the evil one were about the Kingdom of Heaven. Thus, Jesus made it clear from the very beginning that the Kingdom of Heaven was His main concern. He personally took time and used many parables to explain to His disciples and to all of us why it was important for us to first seek the Kingdom of Heaven as

The Kingdom of Heaven

our primary goal and then leave the rest to God who would fulfill all our needs, because He knows them even before we ask for anything. And when Christ sent out His twelve disciples, giving them power to drive out demons and to cure diseases, "he sent them out to preach the kingdom of God and to heal the sick" (Luke 9:2).

Further, Jesus appointed seventy two others and sent them two by two to go ahead of Him to the towns and places he was about to go. As He sent them away, he told them, "The harvest is plentiful but the workers are few. Ask the Lord of the harvest, therefore, to send out workers into the harvest field. Go! I am sending you out like lambs among wolves" (Luke 10:2-3). Jesus' charge to the seventy followers was this: "Heal the sick who are there and tell them 'The kingdom of God is near you'" (Luke 10:9).

It is also remarkable that when Jesus talked about the end of time, He said: **"And this gospel of the kingdom will be preached in the whole world as a testimony to all nations, and then the end will come"** (Mathew 24:14).

He started His Mission talking about the Kingdom of Heaven and continued to present the Kingdom message during His Mission in many parables to His disciples, in the synagogues and to all who gathered around Him. In this chapter, we will explore how the gospel of the Kingdom unfolds during Christ's first coming and how He explained in parables what it takes for us to gain the Kingdom of

The Testimony of Jesus

Heaven. Isn't it wonderful that Christ came to save man so that the sinful man could be redeemed and get back to be with Him in the Kingdom prepared for man at creation? The Kingdom of Heaven has a gate. This gate is Jesus for He said: "I am the way and the truth and the life. No one comes to the Father except through me" (John 14:6). Jesus said: "Because I live, you also will live" (John 14:19). He added: "Whoever has my commands and obeys them, he is the one who loves me. He who loves me will be loved by my Father, and I too will love him and show myself to him" (John 14:21). Whoever loves Christ and opens the door to Him will be received in the Kingdom of Heaven. One can imagine what it will be like on that day when we join Christ in His Kingdom. Christ the King will be full of glory as He sits on the right hand of the Father.

There is every reason why the evil one is focused on preventing people from hearing or retaining anything about the Kingdom of Heaven. His mission is to keep people away from the Kingdom. But he has a hard time with those who hear and retain the word of God. Just like Jesus did, such people would use the scriptures to overcome temptations. Jesus illustrated this in a parable about the farmer who went out to plant seeds: Some seeds fell on the path and the birds ate them, while some fell on rocky places with little soil. Other seeds fell in the thorns and were choked and could not yield fruit. And finally, there were the

The Kingdom of Heaven

seeds which fell on the good soil where they produced much crop – a hundred, sixty or thirty times what was sown (Mathew 13:3-8). Jesus explained this parable. He said that for the one who hears the message about the Kingdom of Heaven and do not understand, "the evil one comes and snatches away what was sown in his heart. This is the seed that was sown along the path" (Mathew 13:19). This is so true. I do not know about you, but for me, I have the hardest time trying to remember any scripture. It seems such an impossible task for as soon as I read or hear the word, I easily forget what I have read. It is just like I read the word "in passing." The interesting thing is that this does not happen with other books or even newspapers that I read. This is why we need to pray as we read God's word and then silently meditate on, and ruminate upon, what we have read.

The next scenario is when the seed falls in a rocky place. Jesus explained that the one who receives the seed that falls in a rocky place is the one "who hears the word and receives it with joy. But since he has no root, he lasts only a short while. When trouble or persecution comes because of the Word, he quickly falls away" (Mathew 13:20-21).

And again this is so true. Those of us who are not rooted in the Word are often quick to fall to temptations. We are quick to blame others and even God for the struggles in our lives.

The Testimony of Jesus

And sometimes when our ways are challenged, for example in our congregations for the things we have done or those we have failed to do, we react negatively and at times run away from our churches.

It is evident that because we are not deeply rooted, we are unlikely to stand firm if we were to face real persecution. But if we were rooted in the Word, we would focus on God and ignore the distractions around us. In the third scenario, Jesus talks about the one who receives the seed that falls in the thorns, who is like the one who hears the Word but "the worries of his life and the deceitfulness of wealth choke it, making it unfruitful." (Mathew 13: 22). We have so many things in our lives which occupy us and prevent the word from germinating in us.

In today's world, the technology has ensured a vast access to secular information and entertainment. The cell phones, the tablets, the computers, the radios and the TVs and the sports are occupying a very big space in our lives. We are held hostage by these gadgets and worldly pleasures and entertainment.

When we go to churches and hear sermons, we do not even remember the topics of sermons, let alone the scriptures which have been read to us. As soon as we are out of a church service, many of us put the various information gadgets to work and we experience direct and conflicting messages and information that choke the Word

The Kingdom of Heaven

planted in us. How then can we expect to be part of God's Kingdom when Jesus returns?

Also, those who are wealthy are included among the ones in whom the Word is choked. Perhaps this is because they get lost in their riches and have little room and space for the germination of the Word. They have no space for the Word of God and their hearts and minds are focused on their riches, making them resistant to the promptings of the Holy Spirit.

Jesus went further to explain the meaning of the seed that fell in good soil. He said: "But the one who received the seed that fell on good soil is the man who hears the word and understands it. He produces a crop, yielding a hundred, sixty or thirty times what was sown" (Mathew 13:23). Those who love the Lord listen to His voice that comes to us through the Holy Spirit.

Jesus has promised us that if anyone hears His voice and opens the door, He will come in and eat with him or her. We are the good soil if we have Christ in us. All that is required of us is to be willing, stop our stubbornness and open the door.

In the book of Mathew chapter 13, Jesus goes to great length to explain what it takes for one to inherit the Kingdom of Heaven or what is needed for us to be part of the kingdom when the end comes. Let me summarize below some of the parables Christ used:

The Testimony of Jesus

- Jesus said that the kingdom of heaven is like a man who sowed good seeds in a field then his enemy came and sowed weeds. When the servant of the owner of the field asked if he could remove the weeds, the owner said "NO" because "while you are pulling the weeds, you may also root up the wheat with them. Let both grow together till harvest" (Mathew 13:29-30).

He explained to His disciples the meaning of the parable of the weeds: He said: "The one who sowed the good seed is the Son of Man. The field is the world, and the good seed stands for the sons of the kingdom. The weeds are the sons of the evil one, and the enemy who sows them is the devil. The harvest is the end of the age, and the harvesters are angels" (Mathew 13:37-39).

Therefore, we are called to be patient with one another and also not to judge each other. Jesus is the judge and will give His judgment at the end of time when he comes with His Kingdom in full glory.

This is when the Son of Man will send out His angels to weed out everything that causes evil and all who do evil will be thrown in the fiery furnace while the righteous ones will inherit the Kingdom of Heaven.

The Kingdom of Heaven

- "The Kingdom of heaven is like a mustard seed, which a man took and planted in his field. Though it is the smallest of all your seeds, yet when it grows, it is the largest of garden plants and becomes a tree, so that the birds of the air come and perch in its branches." And again he said: "The Kingdom of Heaven is like yeast that a woman took and mixed into a large amount of flour until it worked all through the dough" (Mathew 13:31-33). So let us not be afraid to start small when we plant the message of the Kingdom even to unreached places, for the Holy Spirit will take over and ensure that the message spreads everywhere.
- Again Jesus said: "The Kingdom of Heaven is like treasure hidden in a field. When a man found it, he hid it again, and then in his joy went and sold all he had and bought that field (Mathew 13:44).
  Yes, we must search for the Kingdom as it is the greatest treasure anyone can inherit.
- Further, Jesus said: "Again, the Kingdom of Heaven is like a merchant looking for fine pearls. When he found one of great value, he went away and sold everything he had and bought it" (Mathew 13:45).
  When we find Jesus, we must leave worldly things and never look back.

- And Jesus was not finished, for he added: "Once again, the Kingdom of Heaven is like a net that was let down on a lake and caught all kinds of fish. When it was full the fishermen pulled it up on the shore. Then they sat down and collected all the good fish in baskets, but threw the bad away. This is how it will be at the end of age. The angels will come and separate the wicked from the righteous and throw them (the wicked) into the fiery furnace, where there will be weeping and gnashing of teeth" (Mathew 13:47-50). Therefore, as we bring people to Christ, let us not chase away those we consider to be "sinners" and who do not behave the way we expect them to. Let us not be their judge but leave the judgment to Christ who does not want anyone to be lost or be driven away from Him. As it is written, "We who are strong ought to bear with the failings of the weak and not to please ourselves" (Romans 15:1).

Christ came to preach the Kingdom of Heaven, not just by what He said, but by His personal presence on earth. He was from above and knew exactly what He was talking about. The Kingdom of God where Christ came to take us to is a just, peaceful and precious kingdom. There are no words that anyone can use to describe this Kingdom which

The Kingdom of Heaven

is as much spiritual as it is physical. This is a virtual spiritual kingdom that traverses the entire universe with its command centre at the Mercy Seat where the Father sits with Christ at His right hand.

Yet it is also a physical kingdom given the words of Christ when He said that He was going to prepare a place for us and that in His Father's house are many mansions preserved for the victorious elect. It is this Kingdom which the Father has placed under the command and control of Christ our Lord. He rules the Kingdom to the glory of the Father.

Everything Christ did was to make sure that man would be reunited with Him and the Father at the end of time and to be once again part and parcel of the Kingdom. This is why it is so important that the gospel of the Kingdom is spread to the ends of the earth then Christ will return to take His people home. He does not want anyone to be left behind without getting a chance to make a choice after receiving the message of the Kingdom of Heaven.

Further, Jesus said in the Sermon on the Mount, that blessed are the poor in spirit, "for theirs is the Kingdom of Heaven." He added, "Blessed are those who are persecuted because of righteousness, for theirs is the Kingdom of Heaven" (Mathew 5:3, 10).

To be poor in spirit is to accept the Lord and yearn for His Word. It is about surrendering one's will to Christ. It is about accepting that one is a sinner, saved only by grace and grace alone. It is about acknowledging that without God, one is nothing. It is about being hungry for God's Word. It is about dedicating one's life to the service of God. It is about knowing that Christ died for all and shed His blood on the cross to bring back the lost to the Kingdom of God. It is about the willingness to be persecuted because of the truth that is in the word of God. And it is about showing love to all especially the less fortunate. This is what the children of God who are poor in spirit and are seeking His Kingdom are called upon to do. However, we always have an excuse as we often say: "We can only do these things if Christ is in us."

Yes, we can only do them if Christ is in us, but Christ is already willing and is standing at the door. The problem is not on His side, the problem is on our side. So what we should say is something like this: "We can only do these things if we are willing to open the door for Christ to come in and eat with us."

Yes, if we are willing to listen to the Holy Spirit who is counseling us all the time, then our willingness to open the door will be guaranteed. And God knows each one of us and He knows that He has given us the power to choose. So let us stop being stubborn and choose Christ and all these things we will be able to do. But first, let us all acknowledge that we are stubborn and are not allowing Christ to come

The Kingdom of Heaven

into our hearts even when He has told us that He is knocking and ready to come in.

If we truly accept Christ, we will have succeeded in our declared goal to "first seek the Kingdom of Heaven." For by seeking Christ, we seek the Kingdom of Heaven.

Prepare for the kingdom of heaven

As we look forward to our inheritance in the Kingdom of Heaven, let us prepare and be ready. Let us fill our lamps with enough oil. One way of getting us ready for the Kingdom is to actively engage in the end time mission to spread the message of the Kingdom to the ends of the world. This is because as we spread God's word and as we work in His vineyard we grow spiritually. And this can be done at the work place, in the neighborhood, in the social networks and everywhere we go.

Let us be bold and step out without fear, for the Lord will be at our side and will open our minds and speak through us. Let us not leave God's work to the pastors and the clergy alone. This is the time for all Christians to use all the resources available to them to ensure that this message of the coming Kingdom of Heaven penetrates the entire world. And, as we prepare, let us remember that Jesus has called upon us to be humble. This was evident when His disciples asked Him to tell them who is the greatest in the Kingdom of Heaven. Jesus called a little child and had him

The Kingdom of Heaven

stand among them and said: "I tell you the truth, unless you change and become like little children, you will never enter the Kingdom of Heaven. Therefore, whoever humbles himself like this child is the greatest in the Kingdom of Heaven" (Mathew 18:2-4). In a way, it is like Jesus was talking about Himself for he was as humble as a lamb. He was fully God and yet fully human with all the powers and yet He was able to serve with humility?

In a way, Jesus was like a little child. So He was simply telling us to follow in His footsteps and be as humble as He was. Therefore, as we wait for the second coming of Jesus, let us wait in humility.

Also, as we prepare, let us remember the parable of the ten virgins. Jesus said, "At that time the Kingdom of Heaven will be like ten virgins who took their lamps and went out to meet the bridegroom. Five of them were foolish and five were wise.

The foolish ones took their lamps but did not take adequate oil with them. The wise, however, took oil in jars along with their lamps. The bridegroom was a long time in coming, and they all became drowsy and fell asleep" (Mathew 25:1-5). When at midnight the cry rang out: "Here's the bridegroom! Come out to meet him!", all the ten virgins woke up. The foolish ones found out that they did not have enough oil in their lamps and asked the wise ones to give them some. But the wise virgins said a big

The Kingdom of Heaven

"No" and suggested to the foolish ones that they should go and buy more oil for themselves. While they were on the way, the bridegroom arrived. Those virgins who had enough oil went with him to the wedding banquet and then the door to the banquet was shut (Mathew 25:6-10).

When the foolish virgins returned, they found the door shut. "Lord, Lord" they said, "open the door for us!" But he replied, "Truly I tell you, I don't know you" (Mathew 25:11-12). In this parable, the bridegroom is Jesus and the ten virgins are those who have accepted Jesus and all of them are awaiting His second return. Notice that all the ten virgins are asleep after waiting a long time. This is perhaps the same case with us today. We may be asleep but with less oil than is needed. And we may be convinced that we are ready (virgins) to meet Jesus when He comes but then we may not have enough oil in us. The oil here is the Word of God that must be written in our hearts. Let us all make every effort, while there is still time, to get enough oil for the day and the hour of Jesus' return is not known to us and can happen at any time.

We must lead a servant life

As we prepare for the kingdom, let us take a look at what the mother of James and John, the sons of Zebedee, said to Jesus. She came with her two sons, knelt down before the Lord and said: "Grant that one of these two sons of mine may sit at your right and the other at your left in your kingdom" (Mathew 20:21). I believe she was a loving mother who wanted good things for her sons. But in a way, her request was selfish. Jesus responded to her: "You don't know what you are asking." Obviously, she really did not know what she was asking for. Perhaps she was still hoping that Christ will set up an earthly kingdom.

This question by the mother of John led Jesus to call His disciples together to tell them what must be among the most profound teachings we have received from the Lord and which we must ponder as we prepare for the Kingdom of Heaven. Jesus said to them: "You know that the rulers of the Gentiles lord it on them, and their high officials exercise authority. Not so much with you. Instead, whoever wants to become great among you must be your servant, and whoever wants to be first must be your slave – just as the Son of Man did not come to be served, but to serve, and to give his life as a ransom for many" (Mathew 20:25-28).

This is indeed profound.

The Kingdom of Heaven is for those who humble themselves and give up whatever earthly things they have for Christ. We must learn to be servants as Jesus did to us. He assumed a lowly position so that He could relate to us in a more direct way. How wonderful it would be if all of us, including our leaders, led as servants, refraining from showing our powers to all.

The Kingdom of Heaven

It is obvious that the mistake mankind has made is to forget to follow in the footsteps of Jesus. If we did, we would live a servant life and would be humble as we serve the Lord our God. In this way, we would bring more people to know Christ in a deeper way and get to follow Him. Let us read on.

Love and not condemn

Jesus came to show love to all mankind. He loved us and taught us to love one another. He showed us that everyone is somebody. His love for sinners and tax collectors did not go unnoticed by the Pharisees and hypocrites, who complained and wondered why Jesus was mixing with "sinners."

In essence, Jesus taught us to hate sin but love the sinner. This must have been because He knew very well that it is the deceiver who is behind all sins. He also knew that he did not want anyone to be lost.

And Jesus knew that we are all sinners and fall short of God's glory. This is why He came to save us. The savior said: "A new command I give you: Love one another. As I have loved you, so you must love one another. By this everyone will know that you are my disciples, if you love one another" (John 13:34-35).

This love was best illustrated when one day the teachers of the law and the Pharisees brought a woman to Jesus saying: "Teacher, this woman was caught in the act of adultery. In the law Moses commanded us to stone such women. Now, what do you say?" (John 8:4-5). They asked this question so as to trap Jesus and accuse Him of being against the Law of Moses. But the Lord was not about to be trapped.

Instead of giving a straight answer, He bent down and started to write on the ground with His hands. Then He said to them: "Let any one of you who is without sin be the first to throw a stone at her" (John 8:7). He then continued to write on the ground. Everyone who had gathered around left, one by one, until Jesus was left alone with the woman. As they were standing there, the two of them, Jesus said: "Woman, where are they? Has no-one condemned you?" The woman said "No one, sir." Then the Lord said: "Then neither do I condemn you. Go now and leave your life of sin" (John 8:10-11).

The master has no problem with the sinner. He simply wants all sinners to return to Him and be reunited with the Father. This is why He loved sinners so much that He died for all. And, this is why in a parable, He said that suppose one had one hundred sheep and lost one, would he not leave the ninety nine behind and then go look for the lost one. He gave another parable of a woman who had ten coins of silver and lost one. The woman would light a lamp and search everywhere and after she finds the lost coin she would call friends and neighbors to celebrate with her. This is how Jesus wants us to relate to those we think are sinners.

In any case, He has warned us not to be judges as He is the only true and fair judge. And in His own words Jesus said this: "For God did not send his Son into the world to condemn the world, but to save the world through him" (John 3: 17).

Beware of prosperity preaching

We must go to the mountain tops to spread this gospel of the Kingdom of Heaven to the whole world. This is what Christ has asked us to do.

However, the problem in the world today is that many who are supposed to spread this gospel are busy spreading the prosperity gospel and earthly riches.

May be these are the false prophets Christ warned us about. They are more interested in the good life here on earth rather than sacrificial living towards the Kingdom of Heaven.

Many have been deceived and are sometimes being duped into selling their property or giving all they have with the hope that God will pay them back handsomely. They are being asked to plant a "seed" and then wait for a good result and much wealth.

There is nothing wrong with praying for prosperity. There are many verses in the Bible where prosperity is promised to God's children. But as the running theme in this chapter says, we should first seek the Kingdom of Heaven and leave the rest to God who will provide what we need according to His will. For, He is a kind and loving God who causes rain to fall equally to sinners as well as the righteous.

The primary purpose of all Christians should therefore be to prepare people for the Kingdom of Heaven and not to prepare them for earthly enjoyment.

Does it make sense for someone to be prosperous and rich in this earthly life but miss the Kingdom of God? And are we ignoring the scriptures which say that at the time of the end there will be much trouble and anguish in the world including for the elect? This means that the prosperity we seek may in the end be of no use to us.

One of the verses often quoted by prosperity gospel preachers is Jeremiah 29 verse 11 which says: "For I know the plans I have for you." Declares the Lord, "plans to prosper you and not to harm you, plans to give you hope and a future." This is where most people stop.

But this scripture goes on to say in verses 12 and the 13: "Then you will call upon me when you seek me with all your heart. I will be found by you," declares the Lord, "and I will bring you back from captivity."

This passage also applies to us today. The Lord is saying that He has plans to prosper us, but is also asking us to seek

The Kingdom of Heaven

Him with all our hearts. I believe that the prosperity He is promising us is for the common good and not just for selfish gain. There is nothing wrong with prosperity as long as our aim is to glorify God and seek Him unconditionally in all circumstances. I wonder, however, what happens to those who have "planted a seed" and do not get their reward. I also wonder if their intention in planting such a seed is to glorify God and help the needy with whatever they get or just to enrich themselves and satisfy their selfish needs.

Jesus brought this message home when he was sought by a crowd which followed Him and found Him. He said: **"Very truly I tell you, you are looking for me, not because you saw the signs I performed but because you ate the loaves and had your fill."** Jesus added: "Do not work for food that spoils, but for food that endures to eternal life, which the Son of Man will give you. For on Him God the Father has placed His seal of approval" (John 6:26-27). Further, Apostle Paul says in the Book of Romans 11: Vs 35: "Who has ever given God, that God should repay them?"

Vs 36: "For from Him and through Him and for Him are all things. To Him be the glory forever! Amen."

Do we get it?

Treasures in heaven

Now, let us conclude this chapter by looking at the story of the rich young man who one day came to Jesus and asked: "Teacher, what good thing must I do to get eternal life?"

In His reply, Jesus started by referring him to the keeping of the Ten Commandments, mentioning a few.

The rich young man responded saying that he had kept all the commandments and asked: "What do I still lack?" This is when Jesus gave him the answer to his question as He said: "If you want to be perfect, go sell your possessions and give to the poor, and you will have treasure in heaven. Then come, follow me" (Mathew 19:21). On hearing this, the rich young man became sad and walked away from Jesus.

There is no doubt that the rich man's heart was all in his possessions and unless he turned his heart away from his wealth, it was not going to be possible for him to follow Jesus. As the man turned away, Jesus said to His disciples: "Truly I tell you, it is hard for someone who is rich to enter the Kingdom of Heaven. Again I tell you, it is easier for a camel to go through the eye of a needle than for someone who is rich to enter the Kingdom of God" (Mathew 19:23-24).

When the disciples heard this they were astonished and asked: "Who then can be saved?" Jesus said to them: "With

The Kingdom of Heaven

man this is impossible, but with God all things are possible" (Mathew 19:25-26).

Then there was also a certain man who was in one of the crowds that often gathered around Jesus. He said to Jesus, "Teacher, tell my brother to divide the inheritance with me." Jesus replied, "Man, who appointed me a judge or an arbiter between you?"

And He added, "Watch out! Be on your guard against all kinds of greed; **a man's life does not consist in the abundance of his possessions**" (Luke 12:13-15). Soon after Jesus said this, He told the crowd a parable of a "rich fool" who produced good crop and wondered what he would do since he had no more space to store the abundant produce.

The rich man said to himself, "This is what I will do. I will tear down my barns and build bigger ones, and there I will store my grain and my goods. And I will say to myself, 'You have plenty of good things laid up for many years. Take life easy; eat, drink and be merry.'"

"Then Jesus said to him, 'You fool! This very night your life will be demanded from you. Then who will eat what you have prepared for yourself?' And the Master concluded the parable saying, "This is how it will be with anyone who stores up things for himself but is not rich towards God" Luke 12:16-21).

Jesus said that we should not store treasures on earth where moths and vermin would destroy them and where thieves would break in and steal.

But instead we should store our treasures in heaven. He said, "For where your treasure is, there your heart will be also" (Mathew 6:21).

This is a lesson to all those who preach prosperity without first focusing people's minds on the Kingdom of God. For people who become prosperous when they do not know God will be lost in their acquired possessions. Their hearts will be focused on their earthly treasures. So, the only way to be prosperous and still aim for the Kingdom of God is to first seek the kingdom and to give thanks to the Lord Almighty, returning all the tithes and giving much to the poor. There is no need to keep so much in our storehouses when there are many orphans and widows out there and when the House of God is not provided for. And even as we do this, all our hearts should be on heavenly things. This is hard for a rich man to do. Let us spend more time on our knees seeking the Lord and let us invite Christ to be our business partner. This way, all of us will find it easy to go through the eye of a needle.

Be born again

Many of us will need to be born again in Christ as we surrender to Him. We need to have our hearts circumcised

The Kingdom of Heaven

and softened. Jesus had a chance to tell us about being born again when one day He talked to a Pharisee called Nicodemus.

The Pharisee came to Jesus and said, "Rabbi, we know you are a teacher who has come from God. For no-one could perform the miraculous signs you are doing if God were not with him." Jesus said to Nicodemus, "I tell you the truth, no-one can see the kingdom of God unless he is born again" (John 3:1-3).

Obviously Nicodemus did not understand what Jesus meant. He asked, "How can a man be born again when he is old?" And he added, "Surely he cannot enter a second time into his mother's womb to be born again!" (John 3:4). But the Lord went on to explain more to him saying, "I tell you the truth, no-one can enter the kingdom of God unless he is born of water and the Spirit" (John 3:5). Yes, Jesus came to preach the gospel of the Kingdom of Heaven. He came so that we who were lost could rejoin Him and the Father in His eternal kingdom. To be part of this kingdom, we needed to have our hearts circumcised. This would happen when we have the Holy Spirit in us and when we open the door for Jesus to come in and eat with us. If we did this, we would be a new creation, no longer wondering as lost sheep. We would have been born again.

Jesus engaged Nicodemus in a deep discussion which moved the Lord to give us the promise of eternal life

The Testimony of Jesus

written in the book of John chapter 3 verse 16: "For God so loved the world that he gave his one and only Son, that whoever believes in him shall not perish but have eternal life."

Let us remember that God loves us. Because of this, we should focus all our efforts in seeking His kingdom. We should ask God to lead us in this journey and enable us to serve Him and also to be a blessing to others.

When Jesus sent out His twelve disciples, giving them authority to drive out demons and to heal every disease and sickness, He gave them instructions saying: "Do not go among the Gentiles or enter any town of the Samaritans. Go rather to the lost sheep of Israel. As you go, proclaim this message: 'The Kingdom of heaven has come near.' Heal the sick, raise the dead, cleanse those with leprosy, drive out demons. Freely you have received, freely give" (Mathew 10:1-5). These are the words of Jesus. The main charge to His disciples was to "take the message of the Kingdom" first to "Jerusalem" before going to the Gentiles. Similarly, this message of the Kingdom should be preached to all mankind so that they can understand it and participate in spreading it to the rest of the world.

Amen.

CHAPTER 7

CHRIST THE COMPASSIONATE

"Jesus wept." John 11:35

"Take away the stone," the Master commanded. He was about to perform one of the most profound miracles witnessed during His Mission to save the lost. And this is an excellent starting point for this chapter which captures a few of Christ's compassionate acts.

Lazarus, the friend of Jesus, had died some four days past. And Martha and Mary, the sisters of Lazarus, were wailing in disappointment as Jesus did not come to heal their brother "on time." They had sent a message to Jesus saying: "Lord, the one you love is sick" (John 11:3). But Jesus did not go immediately. Instead, He stayed where he was for two more days.

Jesus knew what would happen to Lazarus. For He said: "This sickness will not end in death. No, it is for God's glory so that God's Son may be glorified through it" (John 11:4). In fact, Jesus knew exactly when Lazarus died. He told the disciples: "Our friend Lazarus has fallen asleep; but I am going there to wake him up."

They did not understand that Lazarus had died for they said: "Lord if he sleeps, he will get better." This is when Jesus told them plainly that "Lazarus is dead, and for your sake I am glad I was not there, so that you may believe. But let us go to him" (John 11:11-14).

Let us take a look at what was happening here. Jesus had a friend He loved. He is told that the friend is sick but He does not go immediately for He knew exactly the right time He would intervene. He had purposed that through this death, many including His disciples would believe that He was indeed the Son of God, the Messiah, who was to come. Jesus had a plan.

Now, I have no doubt that this exact situation happens to us all the time. We send a prayer to the Father in the name of Jesus for healing or for whatever we need, then the answer delays and we are disappointed. But this should not be so for the Lord knows when the prayer will be answered. As prophet Isaiah puts it: Woe to those who say, 'Let God hurry, let him hasten his work so that we may see it. Let it approach, let the plan of the Holy One of Israel come, so that we may know it" (Isaiah 5:19). Yes, the Lord is always watching to see that His word is fulfilled (Jeremiah 1:12). So we are called upon to wait patiently and faithfully.

Let us come back to Lazarus. When Jesus arrived in his village of Bethany, Lazarus had been in the tomb for four days.

So when Martha heard that the Lord was on the way, she went out to meet Him and said: "If you would have been here, my brother would not have died." But she still had some faith for she added: "But I know that even now God will give you whatever you ask" (John 11:21-22).

But Jesus comforted Martha and told her that her brother will rise again. This is when Martha revealed her lack of understanding of what Jesus was about to do, as she showed little faith: She said: "I know he will rise again in the resurrection at the last day" (John 11:24).

At this moment Jesus revealed who He really was. He said, **"I am the resurrection and the life. The one who believes in me will live, even though they die; and whoever lives by believing in me will never die. Do you believe this?"** (John 11:25-26). Martha replied: "Yes, Lord, I believe that you are the Messiah, the Son of God, who is to come into the world" (John 11:27).

Now it was Mary's turn to meet the Master. She was informed by Martha that Jesus had arrived. When Mary heard this, she rushed out to meet Jesus. She fell at Jesus' feet and repeated the same sentiments that Martha had expressed, as she said: "Lord if you had been here, my brother would not have died" (John 11:32).

This is when the compassion of Jesus was fully revealed. As He watched Mary and the rest of the people who had gathered cry and mourn for Lazarus, Jesus was deeply moved and asked to be shown where they had laid Lazarus. When He saw the tomb, He cried, as it is written: **"Jesus wept"** (John 11:35).

The Testimony of Jesus

Jesus went to the tomb and said: "Take away the stone" (John 11:39). On hearing this, Martha complained that there must have been a bad smell coming out of the tomb, implying that the stone should not be removed. But Jesus told her, "Did I not tell you that if you believed, you would see the glory of God?" (John 11:40).

Finally, they took away the stone then Jesus said, "Father, I thank you that you have heard me. I know that you always hear me, but I say this for the benefit of the people standing here, that they may believe that you sent me" (John 11:41-42). After He said this, He called out Lazarus from the tomb and the dead man came out walking. Many people who witnessed this believed in Jesus but the Pharisees were afraid of Him and began to plot against Him.

Let us reflect on the major things that occurred. Firstly, Martha and Mary went to meet Jesus. This is relevant to us who are seeking healing and comfort while still on earth and salvation when Jesus returns. We must take that step in faith and come to Jesus.

Secondly, notice that Martha surrenders to Christ and acknowledges Him as the Son of God and the Messiah. This is a lesson to us. Let us surrender our will to Christ and let Him lead.

Thirdly, notice that Jesus who already knew what was to happen (Lazarus would be raised) was still moved when He saw the suffering of Martha and Mary as well as all the mourners. **Yes, Jesus is the compassionate Lord who feels our pain even as He intercedes for us.** He does not want anyone to perish at the end of time. And lastly, let us see what Jesus does next: He said, "Take away the stone."

Of course Jesus could have commanded the stone and it could have rolled itself out of the way. This is also a lesson for us since there are many "stones" that need to be removed even as we await answers from the Lord. These "stones" exist even in those who believe. Lack of faith is one of the big stones. The stones need to be removed. And if they are too heavy, let us ask the Lord to help us remove them.

Jesus showed compassion to many and healed their diseases and their disabilities. He was always quick to say 'your faith has healed you. Go away and sin no more." As we look at the faith of Martha and Mary, let us see the response of a man who brought to Jesus his son who was possessed by a spirit. The man complained to Jesus saying: "Teacher, I brought my son, who is possessed by a spirit that has robbed him of speech. Whenever it sizes him, it throws him on the ground. He foams at the mouth, gnashes his teeth and becomes rigid. I asked your disciples to drive out the spirit, but they could not" (Mark 9:17-18).
Jesus replied: "You unbelieving generation, how long shall I stay with you? How long shall I put up with you? Bring the

The Testimony of Jesus

boy to me" (Mark 9:19). The boy was brought to Him and as soon as the spirit saw Jesus, he threw the boy down with convulsions. When Jesus saw this, He inquired about how long the boy had suffered from the problem. The boy's father explained: "From childhood. It has often thrown him into fire or water to kill him. **But if you can** do anything, take pity on us and help us." Jesus was taken aback by the statement: **"If you can?"** said Jesus. **"Everything is possible for one who believes"** (Mark 9:12-23).

Immediately the boy's father heard what Jesus said, it must have occurred to him that the Master was concerned about his unbelief. So he exclaimed, **"I do believe; help me overcome my unbelief!"** When the compassionate Jesus heard this, he commanded the spirit saying: "You deaf and mute spirit, I command you, come out of him and never enter him again" (Mark 9- 24-25).

This is a powerful testimony of the power Jesus has over demons. We have already seen that He has power over death as He raised Lazarus from the dead. Now, we see Him commanding the evil spirits to go away and never return. And Jesus went on and on healing the sick, the lame and the blind. This was the case when one day a man with leprosy came to Him.

When this leper saw Jesus he fell down on his face and said to the Lord, "If you are willing, you can make me clean" Luke 5:12. Jesus must have felt this man's agony as must have been the case with all lepers who were considered outcasts, not to be touched. Jesus simply told the leper, "I am willing" and added, "Be clean" (Luke 5:13). What is paramount here is that we should never doubt Jesus when we approach Him. We must know that He is able. Yes, my Jesus is able. He has power over death, power over demons and power over everything.

I have often heard fellow believers pray saying to Jesus something like this: "Lord give us travelling mercies. And **if we reach safely we will give you thanks**." Well, with Jesus there is no "IF".

This is the same as saying, "If you can" or "If you are willing". And the problem with those of us, who pray like this, is that we often do not return to the Lord to give any thanks when we reach safely wherever we are going. Obviously, if we pray like this, we shall have not only doubted the Lord but, we shall also have lied about our declared intention to give thanks to Him.

Lord I want to see

One day as Jesus and His disciples were going to the city of Jericho, they met a blind man called Bartimaeus sitting at the road side. When the blind man heard that it was Jesus who was passing, he shouted: "Jesus, Son of David, have mercy on me!" Those who were with Jesus rebuked the blind man telling him to be quiet. I want to imagine that some of them were saying: "Why is this blind man shouting? Does he know who it is that is passing?" Jesus ignored these skeptics and called the blind man to Him (Mark 10: 46-52; Luke 18:35-43).

When the blind man realized that Jesus called him, he threw his cloak aside and jumped to his feet as he went to the Lord who asked him: "What do you want me to do for you?" The blind man answered: "Lord, I want to see." Jesus told him: "Go, your faith has healed you". Immediately the blind man received his sight.

Yes, the compassionate Jesus is asking us even today: "What do you want me to do for you?" We need to tell Jesus this: "Lord, open our eyes so that we may see." Many of us are blind but are unaware of our state. We do not love God enough, but we are unaware. This message was brought home by Jesus to His disciples who asked Him why he was speaking to people in parables. He replied in Mathew 13:11-15:

Vs 11: "Because the knowledge of the secrets of the kingdom of heaven has been given to you, but not to them."

Vs 12: "Whoever has will be given more, and they will have abundance. Whoever does not have, even what they have will be taken from them."

Vs 13: "This is why I speak to them in parables: 'Though seeing, they do not see; though hearing, they do not hear or understand."

Vs 14: "In them is fulfilled the prophecy of Isaiah: 'You will be ever hearing but never understanding; you will be ever seeing but never perceiving."

Vs 15: "For these people's hearts have become calloused; they hardly hear with their ears, and they have closed their eyes. Otherwise they might see with their eyes, and hear with their ears, understand with their hearts and turn, and I would heal them.'"

Jesus can heal our hearts if we are willing to hear His Word. So the greatest gift we should ask of Jesus is for Him to open our eyes so that we can see, and to also open our ears so that we can hear the message of the Kingdom of Heaven. We should ask Jesus to open our eyes to the potential we have in us so that we can use our given gifts to glorify God and to show love to our neighbors. We should use every opportunity to share the testimony of Jesus with others. Again, let us all individually pray this prayer: **"Lord Jesus, open my eyes so that I may see."**

Jesus heals the sick woman

The story of the sick woman who had been bleeding for twelve years shows the healing power of Jesus and His compassion. Just before this marvelous story unfolded, a

The Testimony of Jesus

synagogue leader named Jairus came to Jesus and pleaded with Him to go and heal his dying daughter. As Jesus was on the way to attend to this request, a large crowd gathered and pressed around Him. This is when the sick woman came up behind Jesus in the crowd.

The woman whose name is not given in the Bible had spent all she had seeking care from doctors but the bleeding would not go away.

Because of the faith she had, the woman said to herself, "If I just touch His clothes, I will be healed" (Mark 5:28). What a faith! And indeed, when the suffering woman touched Jesus' cloak she was healed instantly and her bleeding stopped immediately. This is the faith that overcomes the world.

Jesus knew what had just happened because He realized that power had gone out of Him. He then turned around and asked, "Who touched my clothes?" (Mark 31:30).

The disciples were not impressed with this question for they said, "You see the people crowding against you, and yet you ask, 'Who touched me?'" (Mark 31:31).

Ignoring the disciples, Jesus kept looking and behold, the woman came forward and fell at His feet trembling with fear. She told Jesus that she was the one who had touched Him. Jesus simply told her, "Daughter, your faith has healed you. Go in peace and be freed from your suffering" (Mark 5:34). Jesus healed the woman and set her free from her illness. As He did to this woman, so he will do the same to us today.

But wait, the story is not over. Remember that Jesus was actually on His way to heal the daughter of Jairus. While still on the way, news came that Jairus' daughter was already dead. When the people heard this news, they started to cry and were wailing loudly. Jesus told them, "Why this commotion and wailing? The child is not dead but asleep." They did not believe Him and simply laughed. But the Lord was not deterred. He went to the child, took her by the hand and simply said, "Talitha koum!" or "Little girl, I say to you, get up!" And immediately the little girl got up and walked around to the amazement of all who witnessed the miracle (Mark 5:35-42). There is no doubt that all the people witnessing this miracle must have concluded that Jesus was surely "the Son of God, the Messiah."

Jesus feeds thousands

When Jesus heard the news of the death of John the Baptist, He decided to withdraw by boat to a solitary place. But even before Jesus and His disciples reached their destination by boat, crowds had already gathered ahead of them. Jesus saw this large crowd and showed compassion on them, because they were like sheep without a shepherd. As Jesus was teaching the crowd, His disciples noticed that it was getting late in the day. They asked Jesus to send the crowd away so that they could find food to eat. At this point Jesus showed much compassion on the crowd and told the disciples to get some food for the people to eat. The disciples were surprised at the request and said to Jesus that this request needed eight months of a man's salary. Jesus ignored their response and went on to ask them how many loaves of bread they had. They found five loaves and two fish. This was enough for the Master to feed five thousand people. Jesus took the five loaves and two fish. He looked up to heaven and gave thanks and broke the loaves for the disciples to distribute. Everybody ate until they were all full. At the end of the hearty meal, the disciples collected twelve basketfuls of broken pieces of bread and fish (Mathew 14:13-21).

On a separate occasion, Jesus went along the Sea of Galilee and sat on a mountainside. A large crowd gathered around Him. Jesus called His disciples and said to them: "I have compassion for these people; they have already been with me three days and have nothing to eat. I do not want to send them away hungry, or they may collapse on the way" (Mathew 15:32). As was the case when Jesus fed five thousand people, the disciples did not know where they would get food from. Again, Jesus asked them how many loaves of bread they had. They found seven loaves of bread and a few small fish. Jesus told the disciples to get the crowd seated. He gave thanks and then told His disciples to

Christ the Compassionate

distribute the food. About four thousand men ate and were full and afterwards they collected seven basketfuls of broken pieces. Obviously there were more than four thousand people because the number did not include women and children. They all ate and there was a surplus. The compassionate Master provided.

Easting with tax collectors and sinners

Jesus was a friend of sinners. He came to save sinners and not the righteous. So one day, He met a tax collector called Levi sitting at the tax collector's booth. When Jesus told Levi to follow Him, the tax collector did as Jesus said and they then went to eat dinner at Levi's house. They were joined by many other tax collectors and "sinners" (Mark 2:15). The disciples were also there.

When the Pharisees saw this they were not impressed. They asked the disciples why Jesus was eating with tax collectors and sinners. When Jesus heard this, He said to the Pharisees: **"It is not the healthy who need a doctor, but the sick. I have not come to call the righteous, but sinners"** (Mark 2:17).

Another tax collector who Jesus visited was Zacchaeus, a man from Jericho. Zacchaeus was a chief tax collector who was wealthy. He was a short man so he found it difficult to see Jesus amidst a crowd. So he went ahead and climbed a sycamore fig tree so that he could see Jesus.

The Testimony of Jesus

When the Lord saw Zacchaeus, He was pleased with him and said, "Zacchaeus come down immediately. I must stay at your house today" (Luke 19:5).

So Jesus went to be hosted by the chief tax collector. When people saw this they began to mutter saying, 'He has gone to be the guest of a 'sinner'" (Luke 19:7). But Zacchaeus was not deterred. He must have been very happy to host the Lord. He said, "Look, Lord! Here and now I give half of all my possessions to the poor, and if I have cheated anybody of anything, I will pay back four times the amount" (Luke 19:8).

Jesus set the example to us all. Today, many of us are unwilling to go to "sinners." I am aware of a pastor who refused to go and comfort a bereaved family which he considered to have committed some sin. Well, let everyone learn from Christ. It is not enough to just serve the "righteous" for it is we sinners for whom Christ came to die on the cross.

Only one turned back

On another day, as Jesus was travelling to Jerusalem, He went to a village where He met ten men with leprosy. As was expected of lepers, the ten men stood at a distance as they called to Jesus in a loud voice saying, "Jesus, Master, have pity on us!" (17:13). There is no doubt that when such a request reached the compassionate Lord, He could do only one thing: Heal. For, He had seen the suffering of the ten and their hope in Him.

Jesus simply said to the ten lepers: "Go show yourselves to the priests." As they went, they were all cleansed (Luke 17:14). But only one of them, a Samaritan, returned to give thanks to Jesus when he saw that the Lord had healed him. The Samaritan praised God and threw himself at the feet of Jesus.

Jesus asked, "Were not all ten cleansed? Where are the other nine? Has no one returned to give praise to God except this foreigner?" Jesus was pleased with the one who returned and told him: "Rise and go; your faith has made you well." (Luke 17:17-19).

The response of the nine lepers who did not come back to Jesus is a common occurrence. We often forget to give thanks even after receiving what we have asked for, yet we have been told to give thanks in all circumstances whether or not we have received what we have been praying for. After achieving anything in our work, or even before, we often ask for more and more.

We do not remember that the strength, the health and the wisdom to accomplish anything has been freely given to us by God. And after receiving a reward, we do not go back to say "thank you" and do not even return a dime to the Lord. He says to us to return to Him just one tenth of what He has given us to enable God's workers to do His work and to make sure that there is food in God's house and food for the widows, the orphans and the poor, but we do not listen. Sometimes the Lord reminds us through afflictions, loss or trouble. But when He reminds us through afflictions, we sometimes blame Him for trying to wake us up. And many times we lose hope when our afflictions do not go away as fast as we would like it to be. Well, let us learn to always trust the Lord.

Healing the widow's only son

One day Jesus went to a town called Nain. As usual, a large crowd followed Him. As He approached the town, there was a dead person being carried. This was the only son of his mother who was a widow. Jesus saw what was happening and He had compassion over the woman. Jesus went and touched what the dead man was being carried on and said, "Young man, I say to you, get up!" (Luke 7:14).

The young man got up immediately and began to talk. The boy's mother must have been in shock and wondered how this could happen. To get her dead son back was the greatest gift she could have hoped for. The news about this miracle spread widely and many people believed in Jesus as the Son of God. Let us note that in this particular healing, no one had asked Jesus to do anything. He acted without being asked as he always does. He will do the same to us today. Jesus performed many miracles. It is not the purpose of this chapter to highlight all of them. I have selected just a few to illustrate how compassionate our Lord and Savior is. Let us wait on the Lord for He is good and compassionate. As it is written in the book of Isaiah chapter 30 verse 18: "The Lord longs to be gracious to you; He rises to show you compassion. For the Lord is a God of justice. Blessed are all who wait for Him."

Who is my neighbor?

The parable of the Good Samaritan is one of the greatest messages Jesus shared with us. This parable was in response to a simple question asked by an expert of the law who said to Jesus, "What must I do to inherit eternal life?" (Luke 10:25).

The expert was actually testing Jesus but the Lord turned everything around and instead of answering the expert, He simply asked him to state what the law said about this question.

The expert went ahead and quoted from scriptures saying, "Love the Lord your God with all your heart and with all your soul and with all your strength and with all your mind" and "Love your neighbor as yourself" (Luke 10:27).

Jesus told him that he gave the correct answer and said to the expert, "Do this and you will live" (Luke 10:28). But the expert was not finished. He asked Jesus, "And who is my neighbor?" (Luke 10:29). Instead of giving any more direct answers, Jesus turned to the Parable of the Good Samaritan.

Jesus related the story of one who was travelling from Jerusalem to Jericho and met robbers who stripped him of his clothes, beat him up and left him for dead.

A priest was going down the same road but ignored the injured man. The priest simply passed on the other side of the road. Then a Levite also came and, as the priest did, he passed on the other side of the road. The "men of God" showed no compassion on the injured person and simply walked away.

And then a Samaritan who had pity on him appeared. He cared for the injured man, bandaged his wounds and then carried him on a donkey to an inn. The Samaritan stayed until the next day and gave the inn-keeper money so that he could continue caring for the injured man. The Samaritan also promised to come back and reimburse any additional expenses the inn would incur.

At this point, Jesus asked the law expert, "Which of these three do you think was a neighbor to the man who fell into the hands of robbers?" The expert answered, "The one who had mercy on him" (Luke 10:36-38). Jesus told the expert to go and do the same to others in need. Today, the compassionate Lord is also asking us to go out there and do the same.

Christ the Compassionate

By His stripes we are healed

Jesus is the same yesterday, today and tomorrow. His compassionate love is forever. Today, He is still in the healing business. As it is written, Jesus carried our sins in His body on the cross and that by His stripes or wounds we are healed (1 Peter 2:24). The Lord is indeed is the God of justice. Therefore, let us patiently wait for Him.

The compassionate Lord is willing to carry our burdens. Let us also be willing to open the doors of our hearts so that He can come in and eat with us.

CHAPTER 8

COME AND DRINK FROM THE SPRING OF THE LIVING WATER

"Come to me, all you who are weary and burdened, and I will give you rest." Mathew 11:28

I would like to take a different tone as we come into this chapter. We have so far seen the Testimony of Jesus as it unfolds. There is no doubt whatsoever who Jesus is. He is the Son of Man, the Wonderful counselor, the Savior and Redeemer. He is God the Son who sits at the right hand of God the Father. He is the one with whom and through whom the Father created the heavens and earth. He is the King of Kings under whom everything has been put by the Father. He is the Alpha and the Omega. He is our intercessor and our High Priest now interceding for us in the Heavenly Sanctuary. He is also the one who will judge the world for He says the Father does not judge anyone as all judgments have been committed to Him. And, He is the one who has personally preached the end-time message of the Kingdom of Heaven saying loudly, "Repent, for the Kingdom of Heaven is near."

And He is the same Jesus who will come again to take us home.

Come and Drink from the Spring of the Living Water

Now, Jesus is calling us to come to Him, for He is the spring of the living water. He is calling us to come and surrender to Him. Let us come and acknowledge Him as our Lord and Savior. Let us come to Him while there is still time as we look forward to His second coming. Let us come to the spring of the living water so that we will never thirst again. And let us come, for the savior is standing at the door and knocking, eager to enter into our hearts. He is pleading with us daily. So, let us open our hearts to Him. Jesus knows that we are sinners and that is why He is calling us to come as we are.

Even before we read what happened at the Cross in the next chapter, there is more than enough testimony of Jesus in the Bible for us to take a stand. Yes, more than enough. **So what more evidence are we waiting for?** Or are we fulfilling the prophecy in the book of Prophet Isaiah that said: "You will be ever hearing but never understanding; you will be ever seeing but never perceiving?" (Isaiah 6:9). Are we? And let me be personal here: Are you? If you are not, and if you have been reading this Testimony of Jesus up to this point, I want you to think again about the whole Testimony of Jesus. And I am also included in this call.

Yes, let us take a stand for Jesus. Let us repent for the Kingdom of Heaven is near. This we must all do. But wait a minute. For even as we struggle with this decision, let us see how the people who witnessed the things we have described

The Testimony of Jesus

in the foregoing chapters responded during the time Jesus was here on earth, in His first coming to save the world. As Jesus continued His Mission, He was saddened by the response in the towns in which He had performed many miracles for they did not repent. He lamented, as it is written, that if the miracles He performed in such towns as Bethsaida had been performed in Tyre and Sidon, they would have repented. And He added that if the miracles performed in Capernaum were performed in Sodom, the story would have been different.

And in His own words, Jesus said of Capernaum: "And you, Capernaum, will you be lifted to the heavens? No, you will go down to Hades. For, if the miracles that were performed in you had been performed in Sodom, it would have remained to this day. But I tell you that it will be more bearable for Sodom on the Day of Judgment than for you" (Mathew 11:23-24).I know that we are all stubborn and many of us just read or hear God's word and then pass on to other things. This time it must be different.

Just as Jesus warned us (Luke 17:26-28), let it not be like the days of Noah when people went on eating, drinking and marrying ignoring the warnings until the doors of the Ark were closed. And let it not be like in the days of Lot when people refused to listen and were burnt up in Sodom. Now, Jesus Himself has told us: "Repent for the Kingdom of Heaven is near" and that the hour is not known.

Come and Drink from the Spring of the Living Water

Yes, the Lord can come at any time since we are living in borrowed time. Let us accept this message and be watchful as we await The Second Coming. While we still have time, let us not wait but come and drink from the spring of the living water. Let us come to Jesus, to the glory of the Father.

The Lord is not happy if one sinner dies. And the Lord shows His concern, as it is written in the book of Jeremiah 2:13, "My people have committed two sins: They have forsaken me, the spring of the living water, and have dug their own cisterns, broken cisterns that cannot hold water." And in the book of Ezekiel the Lord declares: "Do I take any pleasure in the death of the wicked? Rather, am I not pleased when they turn from their ways and live?" (Ezekiel 18:23).

Our God is a good God. For, it is written in 1 Chronicles 16:34 that we should: "Give thanks to the Lord, for he is good; his love endures forever." He is a patient and loving God. He will not give up on us and that is why Jesus died on the cross to save us.

Yes, the Lord is good. And it is also written: "Taste and see that the Lord is good; blessed is the one who takes refuge in him." (Psalm 34:8).

Therefore, He will still forgive us. And that is why when Peter went to Jesus and asked, "Lord how many times shall I forgive my brother or sister who sins against me? Up to seven times?" Jesus replied, "I tell you, not seven times, but seventy times seven" (Mathew 18:21-22).

Jesus then went on to tell the parable of the unmerciful servant who was forgiven his debts only to turn and refuse to do the same to a fellow servant who owed him much less than he had owed his master. So the master was outraged and handed the servant over to the jailers so that he could pay all he owed.

So Jesus said:

> "This is how my heavenly Father will treat each of you unless you forgive your brother or sister from your heart" (Mathew 18:35). But having said this, we should be careful not to grieve the Holy Spirit.

In the book of Hebrews 6:4-6, it is written: "It is impossible for those who have once been enlightened, who have tasted the heavenly gift, who have shared in the Holy Spirit, who have tasted the goodness of the word of God and the powers of the coming age and who have fallen away, to be brought back to repentance. **To their loss they are crucifying the Son of God all over again subjecting him to public disgrace.**"

In spite of this, let us not be judge of ourselves or of others for we know that with God ALL things are possible. And, as we come to the spring of the Living Water, let us remember to be humble and to forgive others as we have been forgiven.

Come and Drink from the Spring of the Living Water

"Come see a man"

One day, Jesus sat down by a well. This well was called Jacob's well for it was near a plot of the ground that Jacob had given to Joseph his son. This was in a town in Samaria known as Sychar.

As Jesus sat there, a Samaritan woman who had gone to the well to draw water appeared. When Jesus saw her, He asked her for water saying, "Will you give me a drink?" (John 4:7).

A conversation started between Jesus and the woman as is written in the Book of John chapter 4:

Vs 9: "The Samaritan woman said to him, "You are a Jew and I am a Samaritan woman. How can you ask me for a drink?" (For Jews do not associate with Samaritans).

Vs 10: "Jesus answered her, 'If you knew the gift of God and who it is that asks for a drink, you would have asked him and he would have given you living water.'"

Vs 11: "'Sir,' the woman said, 'you have nothing to draw with and the well is deep. Where can you get this living water?'"

Vs 12: "Are you greater than our father Jacob, who gave us the well and drank from it himself, as did also his sons and livestock?"

Vs 13: "Jesus answered, 'Everyone who drinks this water will be thirsty again,'" Vs 14: "but whoever drinks the water I give them will never thirst. Indeed, the water I give them will become in them a spring of water welling up to eternal life."

This is one of the greatest conversations recorded about Jesus talking one-on-one with someone about Himself as the Spring of Living Water. He is the living water from which we will never thirst. And this conversation is so captivating that we must read the whole of it.

The woman said to Jesus: "Give me some of the water so that I won't get thirsty and have to keep coming here to draw water." Obviously she did not understand what Jesus was telling her and one cannot blame her.

So for Jesus to drive the message home, He decided to use another method, one that would reveal who He really was. So He asked the woman to tell Him who her husband was, knowing very well that she did not have one.

And when she told Jesus that she had none, Jesus told her that she answered correctly and then went ahead to tell her details of what she really was and that she'd had five husbands previously. At this point the woman realized who she was dealing with and said, "I can see that you are a prophet."

In John chapter 4 verses 21 - 24, it is written:

Come and Drink from the Spring of the Living Water

"Woman," Jesus replied, "believe me, a time is coming when you will worship the Father neither on this mountain nor in Jerusalem. You Samaritans worship what you do not know; we worship what we do know, for salvation is from the Jews. Yet a time is coming and has now come when the **true worshipers will worship the Father in the Spirit and in truth**, for they are the kind of worshipers the Father seeks.

God is spirit, and his worshipers must worship in Spirit and truth." The woman said to Jesus: "I know that the Messiah (called Christ) is coming. When he comes, he will explain everything to us." Then Jesus declared, **"I, the one speaking to you – I am he"** (John 4:25-26).

On hearing this, the woman left the well and went back to her town. She even left her water jar behind. On reaching the town she called the people: "**Come see a man** who told me everything I ever did. Could this be the Messiah?" (John 4:29). The message spread and many Samaritans believed.

This is a remarkable story, full of action and revelation. Jesus chose to sit at the well, waiting once more to reveal Himself to us. And He must have known in advance that the Samaritan woman would be going to the well. And what a place He chose - Jacob's well. He was waiting to give a testimony about Himself. Christ chose this occasion to deliver one of His most powerful teachings. He said that a time was coming when true worshipers will worship the

The Testimony of Jesus

Father in the Spirit and in truth, for they are the kind of worshipers the Father seeks. God is spirit, and his worshipers must worship in Spirit and truth. It is at the well that Jesus again identified Himself as the Messiah for He told the woman, "I, the one speaking to you – I am he."

I want to imagine that as soon as the woman realized that she had actually seen the Messiah, she became very excited and started running back to her town. People must have looked at her and wondered what had happened to her. But all that was in her mind must have been the Messiah. She became a powerful witness and gave a testimony of her experience with Jesus.

It is not surprising, therefore, that many Samaritans in that town believed in Jesus because of the woman's testimony. Jesus stayed two more days in the town resulting in many more believing in Him. The people of the town said to the woman: "We no longer believe just because of what you said; now we have heard for ourselves, and we know that this man really is the Savior of the world" (John 4:42).

Now, let me come back to the question: **"With all this evidence, what are we waiting for?"** And if you have read up to this point, I would like you to ask yourself this question: **"What I am waiting for?** The time is now. Let us accept Jesus as our Lord and savior to the glory of God our Father. I want to suggest that we stop for a short prayer.

Come and Drink from the Spring of the Living Water

Let us pray this prayer:

> Lord Jesus, I do believe that you are the Son of the living God. You are the Messiah, my Savior and Redeemer. Come into my heart. I now surrender. Give me the water from which I will never thirst again. Amen.

Jesus is the bread of life

Jesus, the spring of the living water, is also the bread of life. Jesus identified Himself as the bread of heaven as we read in John chapter 6 verses 26- 51. In these verses Jesus was talking to a crowd that had gathered to see Him. Jesus said to them: "Do not work for food that spoils, but for food that endures to eternal life, which the Son of Man will give you. For on Him God the Father has placed his seal of approval" (John 6:27).

On hearing this they asked Jesus, "What must we do to do the works God requires?" (John 6:28). Jesus answered them that "the work of God is to believe in the one he has sent." These stubborn people demanded a miracle from Jesus so that they could believe in Him. They reminded Jesus of the miracle of manna that the children of Israel ate as they fled Egypt. At this point Jesus must have been getting concerned about them for he said, "I tell you the truth, it is not Moses who gave you the bread from heaven, but it is my Father who gives you the true bread from heaven. For the bread of God is he who comes down from heaven and gives life to the world" (John 6:32-33). When He said this, the people in the crowd told Him: "Sir, from now on give us this bread." On hearing this Jesus declared: "I am the bread of life. He who comes to me will never go hungry, and he who believes in me will never be thirsty" (John 6:34-35).

What more can we say. Jesus has said it all. He is the spring of the living water and he is the bread of life that came down from heaven to reclaim the lost. For in His own words, He said: "For I have come down from heaven not to do my will but to do the will of him who sent me. And this is the will of him who sent me, that I shall lose none of all those he has given me, but raise them up at the last day. For my Father's will is that everyone who looks to the Son and believes in him shall have eternal life, and I will raise them up at the last day" (John 6:38-40).

What a promise! And how can anyone refuse such a gift of life that is guaranteed in Jesus? How? At this point, I want to return to the question: **"If this is what Jesus Himself is saying – not any pastor or any evangelist – then what are we waiting for?"** Shall we continue to be stubborn as in the days of Lot and Noah? Or are we ready to open our hearts for Jesus to come in and do the rest for us? Remember, He says that He is ready and is standing at the door, knocking. And remember that salvation is not by our own effort, but by grace and grace alone. What we have been called to do is to simply take the step, have faith and believe in Jesus to the glory of God the Father. We need to remind ourselves again and again that we must be willing to open the door for the spring of the living water to come in and fill us.

The Father is the Gardener

Jesus said that He is the vine and we are the branches of the vine. And that the Gardener is the Father (John 15:1). He went on to say that the Father prunes every branch that bears fruit so that it can bear more fruit while those branches that do not bear fruit are cut off from the vine. Let us read what Jesus says in John 15:5-17.

Vs 5: "I am the vine; you are the branches. If you remain in me and I in you, you will bear much fruit; apart from me you can do nothing."

Vs 6: "If you do not remain in me, you are like a branch that is thrown way and withers; such branches are picked up, thrown into fire and burned."

Vs 7: "If you remain in me and my words remain in you, ask whatever you wish, and it will be done for you."

Vs 8: "This is to my Father's glory, that you bear much fruit, showing yourselves to be my disciples."

Vs 9: "As the Father has loved me, so have I loved you. Now remain in my love."

Vs 10: "If you keep my commands, you will remain in my love, just as I have kept my Father's commands and remain in his love."

Vs 11: "I have told you so that my joy may be in you and that your joy may be complete. My command is this: **Love each other as I have loved you**. Greater love has no one than this: to lay down one's life for one's friends."

Vs 14: "You are my friends if you do what I command."

Vs 15: "I no longer call you servants, because a servant does not know his master's business.

"Instead, I have called you friends, for everything that I have learnt from my Father I have made known to you."

Vs 16: "You did not choose me, but I chose you and appointed you so that you might go and bear fruit – fruit that will last – and so that whatever you ask in my name the Father will give you."

Vs 17: "This is my command: Love one another."

Wow! Jesus has spoken. And His words are sweet. So sweet that all I could do is to let the Bible speak to you in the words of Jesus, uncut. For, there is no way one can say what Jesus is saying here in any other words. These words are in the Bible. However, many people do not have Bibles and even those who have them do not often read them. It is therefore imperative that at every opportunity, the word of God must be disseminated to all. Jesus says that if He had not spoken to us, we would not be guilty of sin. Let us read this in His own words in John 15:22-25: "If I had not come and spoken to them, they would not be guilty of sin; but now they have no excuse for their sin."

Vs 23: "Whoever hates me hates my Father as well."

Vs 24: "If I had not done among them the works no one else did, they would not be guilty of sin. As it is, they have seen, and yet they have hated both me and my Father."

Vs 25: "But this is to fulfill what was written in their law: They hated me without reason." These words are so profound.

They are the words of one who is pleading with people He really loves. The words of one who does not want anyone to die in sin, One who wants to redeem us all. Yes, this is the One who loves us unto death. How else could anyone plead to a friend? How else could anyone seek the very best – the Kingdom of Heaven – for a friend who despises him or her the way Jesus was despised? How else?

The Testimony of Jesus

In what other way could Jesus have talked to us? So why should we not repent and come to Him?
Why?

The counselor

Jesus did not stop here because He knows us. He is very much aware that we are forgetful and stubborn. So when He was about to go away, He made sure that we are not left alone as orphans. He said in John 14:16-18: "And I will ask the Father, and he will give you another advocate to help you and be with you forever – the Spirit of truth.

The world cannot accept him, because it neither sees nor know him. But you know him, for he lives in you and will be in you. I will not live you as orphans; I will come to you." And in John 15:26, Jesus said: "When the advocate comes, whom I will send to you from the Father – the Spirit of truth who goes out from the Father – he will testify about me."

After Jesus ascended, following the resurrection, His disciples gathered in Jerusalem and joined together in prayer. And they were together when the day of Pentecost came. As they sat in a house, they suddenly heard a sound like the blowing of a violent wind. This sound filled the house and they saw what looked like tongues of fire which separated and came to rest on each one of them. It was the Holy Spirit who came and filled them. They then started to speak in tongues. Unlike the speaking in tongues of today, everyone who heard the disciples speak could hear what they were saying in their respective languages. Indeed, as Christ promised, the Holy Spirit was sent down from the Father.

Yes, the Holy Spirit is with us always, showing us the way and counseling us all the time. However, many times we are too busy with the things of the world which occupy us making it difficult for us to listen to the Holy Spirit. The cell phones, the tablets, the never ending music and entertainment, the television, the love of money and the search for pleasures of this world keep us busy and cloud our judgment making it even more difficult for us to hear what the Holy Spirit is telling us. The good news is that He will not give up on us as God does not want us sinners to die but to seek His Kingdom.

Life in abundance

Jesus the spring of the living water and the bread of life said that He came so that we may have life and have it abundantly (John 10:10). This is so true. For when we seek the Kingdom of Heaven with all our hearts and with all our minds, when we believe in Jesus as the Messiah, Lord and Savior and when we open the doors of our hearts for Jesus to come in and eat with us, there is only one outcome and that is abundant life.

The Testimony of Jesus

We have been told to "Taste and see that the Lord is good; blessed is the one who takes refuge in him" (Psalm 34:8). Those who accept Jesus as their Lord and Savior will experience fulfillment in life to the extent that they may begin to wonder why they wasted much time before coming to Him. They will experience abundance in life no matter what their situation is and will have joy in each and every situation.

Jesus warns us not to worry about our lives for He says: "Therefore I tell you, do not worry about your life, what you will eat or drink or about your body, what you will wear. Is not life more than food and the body more than clothes? "Look at the birds of the air; they do not sow or reap or store away in burns, and yet your heavenly Father feeds them. Are you not much more valuable than they? Can any one of you by worrying add a single hour to your life?" (Mathew 6:25-27).

In his letter to Timothy, the Apostle Paul says:

> "But godliness with contentment is great gain. For we brought nothing into this world, and we can take nothing out of it" (1 Timothy 6:6-7).

Therefore, let us accept God no matter what circumstances we find ourselves in. When we seek prosperity, this should not be for selfish ends but for common good.

Come and Drink from the Spring of the Living Water

Those who are prosperous need to be channels of blessings to the less fortunate. If we do not do this, the wealth we have will bring many temptations that may lead us to sin.

Do not serve two masters

Jesus told us that it is not possible for one to serve two masters at the same time. He said, "No one serves two masters. Either you will hate the one and love the other, or you will be devoted to the one and despise the other. You cannot serve God and money" (Luke 16:13).

In the book of Ecclesiastes, it is written that: "Whoever has money never has enough; whoever loves wealth is never satisfied with their income...." (Ecclesiastes 5:10).

The book of Ecclesiastes adds that, "Everyone comes naked from their mother's womb; and as everyone comes, so they depart. They take nothing from their toil that they can carry in their hands" (Ecclesiastes 5:15). This is so true. However, it does not mean that we should not work hard and be prosperous in what we do. The common thread must be that those who are blessed should be channels that God uses to serve Him and to show compassion to the less fortunate.

The Bible also calls upon us not to prostitute ourselves with other gods. Because when we do so we are serving two masters. In the book of Revelation, we are called to come out of Babylon. We are called to leave worldly things and keep our eyes on the Lord. John the revelator wrote in Revelation 14:6:

"Then I saw another angel in mid-air, he had the eternal gospel to proclaim to those who live on the earth – to every nation, tribe, language and people. He said in a loud voice, 'Fear God and give him glory, because the hour of his judgment has come. Worship him who made the heavens, the earth, the sea and the springs of water."

This call is for all mankind to worship God and God alone. It is a call to worship God as the creator. We cannot have any other gods. Let us leave the things of the world and heed the cry of another angel who spoke to John saying in Revelation chapter 18:

Vs 2: "With a loud voice he shouted: "Fallen, fallen is Babylon the great! She has become a home for demons and a haunt for every evil spirit, a haunt for every unclean and detestable bird."

Vs 3: "For all the nations have drunk the maddening wine of her adultery. The kings of the earth committed adultery with her, and the merchants of the earth grew rich from her excessive luxuries."

Then John heard another angel saying: "Come out of her, my people, so that you will not share in her sins, so that

Come and Drink from the Spring of the Living Water

you will not receive any of her plagues; for her sins are piled up to heaven and God has remembered her crimes" (Revelation 18:4).

We must come out of Babylon by the grace of God. We must leave the confusion and the pleasures of the world. We must not prostitute ourselves by refusing to keep the commandments of God. And, we must hold on to the testimony of Jesus.

To the church of Laodicea, Jesus said that He rebukes and disciplines those He loves and called upon all to repent. He said: "To him who overcomes, I will give the right to sit with me on my throne, just as I overcame and sat down with my Father on his throne" (Revelation 3:21). However, He cautioned those who serve two masters. He said, "I know your deeds, that you are neither cold nor hot. I wish you were either one or the other. So because you are lukewarm – neither hot nor cold – I am about to spit you out of my mouth" (Revelation 3:15-17).

These are strong words indeed. But the Lord is good. He is all powerful, yet merciful and kind. He will not give us a burden we cannot carry. As the Lord told the children of Israel, so He is telling us today that He will put His laws in our minds and write them in our hearts so that He will cause us to follow Him.

Jesus is standing at the door and is waiting for us to open our hearts so that He can come in and eat with us. Let us pray that we grow in Christ each day as we prepare for His second coming. Above all, let us repent for the Kingdom of Heaven is near. And let us go to the spring of the living water and drink so that we shall never be thirsty again. For the Lord told John the Revelator this: "It is done.

I am the Alpha and the Omega, the Beginning and the End. To the thirsty I will give water without cost from the spring of life. Those who are victorious will inherit all this, and I will be their God and they will be my children" (Revelation 21:6-7).

In the Book of Isaiah, the Lord says: "Come, all you who are thirsty, come to the waters; and you who have no money, come buy and eat! ..." (Isaiah 55:1). As it is written, let us seek the Lord while He may be found and call on Him while he is near (Isaiah 55:6). To God be the glory forever and ever. Amen.

CHAPTER 9

AT THE CROSS

"I am the good shepherd. The good shepherd lays down his life for the sheep." John 10:11

The time had come. And the Father was sitting on His throne, alone. For, He had sent forth His Son into the lost world. Jesus was about to fulfill the plan that had been hatched out before Adam and Eve had sinned. As this was unfolding, the heavens remained sad and happy all at the same time: Sad because the Son of Man, in His pending death on the cross, was about to suffer severe but temporary separation from the Father; and happy because time had now come to make it possible for sinful men and women to be reunited with the Father through Jesus.

This death on the cross was not just another death. For, it was the death of the Son of God, the ultimate sacrifice by the Father. Let us stop just for a moment here. How could the King of Kings, the one through whom the Father created the heavens and the earth, the Son of man who sits at the right hand of the God, the one under whom everything had been placed by the Father including those who were spiting on Him and abusing Him – the people for whom He came to die and to save – humble Himself and accept to be ridiculed, tortured and be put to shame as was the case before His death on the cross? How could this be possible when Christ had power over death? How? How precious are we that Christ could die for us? And, why did He have to die in the manner in which He was killed on the cross?

The answer to these questions is in one word, LOVE. And this is why it is written in John 3:16 that: "For God so loved the world that He gave His one and only Son, that whoever believes in Him shall not perish but have eternal life." Yes, Jesus came from the Father to save the lost.

As the end of His Mission approached, Jesus took His twelve disciples aside and said to them: "We are going to Jerusalem and everything that is written by the prophets about the Son of Man will be fulfilled. He will be turned over to the Gentiles. They will mock him, insult him, spit on him, flog him and kill him. On the third day he will rise again" (Luke 18:31-33).

Obviously, the disciples did not understand what Jesus was talking about. But the Master had thus forewarned them of what was to come: His eminent death on the cross that would be preceded by insults, flogging and spitting of saliva on Him. It was in a house in Bethany, the town where Lazarus had been raised from the dead, where Jesus and His disciples had dinner. Lazarus was among those at the table. His sister Martha served as his other sister, Mary Magdalene, took an expensive perfume and poured it on

At the Cross

Jesus feet. She went further to wipe His feet with her hair (John 11:3). His disciples were surprised. One of them, Judas Iscariot who was the betrayer of Jesus said, "Why wasn't this perfume sold and the money given to the poor?" (John 11:5). Jesus rebuked Judas telling him to leave Mary alone, adding: "It was intended that she should save this perfume for the day of my burial. You will always have the poor among you, but you will not always have me" (John 11:7-8).

Jesus knew that the time had come for Him to fulfill His Mission. He was ready to die, but His disciples were still grappling with the whole idea and did not understand what the Master was telling them.

Prayers

Jesus was prepared to suffer all the humiliation for us. He decided that He was going to remain as silent as a lamb even at the height of this provocation and insubordination. He spent time with His disciples preparing them for what was to come and praying with them.

One of the most powerful prayers was for Peter well in advance of Peter's impending denial of Jesus. The Savior told Peter: "Simon, Simon, Satan has asked to sift you as wheat. But I have prayed for you, Simon, that your faith may not fail. And when you have turned back, strengthen your brothers" (Luke 22:31-32). Peter must have been taken aback for he knew nothing of the impending temptation. All he knew was that he was very committed to Jesus and could not do such a thing as denying the Lord. Peter said: "Lord, I am ready to go with you to prison and to death" (Luke 22:34).

But Jesus went ahead to explain to him that before the rooster crowed on that night, Peter would deny Him three times. And indeed, Peter denied Jesus three times as Jesus had told him.

The prayer for Peter is a beautiful testimony for us so that we can be certain that our intercessor and Friend is praying for us even before we fall into temptation, for He knows well ahead of time everything that is going to happen to us.

He is praying for us even when we do not know and even when we have no idea that He is doing so. What a wonderful Savior! Before His arrest, Jesus prayed for Himself saying in John chapter 17:

vs 1, "Father, the hour has come. Glorify your Son, that your Son may glorify you.

Vs 2: For you granted Him authority over all people that He might give eternal life to all those you have given Him.

Vs 3: Now this is eternal life: that they know you, the only true God, and Jesus Christ, whom you sent.

Vs 4: I have brought you glory on earth by finishing the work you gave me to do.
Vs 5: And now, Father glorify me in your presence with the glory I had with you before the world began."

Then Jesus prayed for His disciples. In His prayer, Jesus acknowledged that the disciples had been obedient and had received knowledge from Him. None had been lost except the one who would betray Him. He said:

> "I have given them your words and the world hates them, for they are not of the world any more than I am of the world. My prayer is not that you take them out of the world but that you protect them from the evil one. They are not of the world, even as I am not of it" (John 17:14-16).

Jesus was not finished. He turned His attention to the believers. This prayer to all believers is powerful and I would like to just put it down as it was so that we can all be blessed by it – John 17:20-26: Vs 20: "My prayer is not for them (disciples) alone. I pray also for those who will believe me through their message,"

Vs 21: "that all of them may be one, Father, just as you are in me and I am in you. May they also be in us so that the world may believe that you have sent me."

Vs 22: "I have given them the glory that you gave me, that they may be one as we are one,"

Vs 23: "I in them and you in me – so that they may be brought to complete unity. Then the world will know that you sent me and have loved them as you have loved me."

Vs 24: "Father, I want those you have given me to be with me where I am, and to see my glory, the glory you have given me because you loved me before the creation of the world."

Vs 25: "Righteous Father, though the world does not know you, I know you, and they know that you have sent me."

Vs 26: "I have made you known to them, and I will continue to make you known in order that the love you have for me may be in them and that I myself may be in them."

This is a prayer of a shepherd who loves his sheep. A shepherd who is ready to snatch a lamb from the jaws of a lion, a shepherd who will do everything to find water so that all his sheep would drink and quench their thirst and a shepherd who will provide a shelter for all his sheep. This is the shepherd who will leave the ninety nine sheep he has and go looking for the one lost sheep until he finds it and brings it back to the den. Our Lord and Savior is the good shepherd.

Jesus is arrested

After these prayers, Jesus left with His disciples and went to the place where He would be arrested. Judas was there to lead soldiers and some officials from the Chief Priest as well as some Pharisees to the place as he already knew where Jesus would be.

When the soldiers got to the place, Jesus asked them who they were looking for and they replied that they wanted Jesus of Nazareth. The Lord quickly told them, "I am he." As He said this, those who came to arrest Him drew back and fell to the ground.

I want to imagine that as this was happening the disciples must have been terrified. Peter stepped up ready to defend the Lord. He drew his sword and cut off the ear of a servant of the High Priest. But the Lord was not impressed by what Peter did. He told Peter, "Put your sword away! Shall I not drink the cup the Father has given me?" (John 18:11).

After this, the soldiers arrested Jesus, bound Him and took Him to Annas, the father-in-law of the high priest. Jesus was questioned about His disciples and about His teachings. His answer to the High Priest was: "I have spoken openly to the world. I have always taught in synagogues or at a temple, where all the Jews come together. I said nothing in secret. Why question me? Ask those who heard me. Surely they know what I said." On hearing this, one of the officials slapped Him in the face saying: "Is this how you answer the high priest?" (John 18:20-22).

Now, how can anyone slap anybody for the innocent response Jesus gave to the question put to Him? I suppose that the one who slapped Jesus did not know what he was doing. But Jesus was not about to overreact to this provocation. He simply said: "If I said something wrong, testify as to what is wrong. But if I spoke the truth, why did you strike me?" (John 18:23-24).

At this point Annas decided to send Jesus to Caiaphas the high priest. From there He was taken to Pilate, the Roman governor. Jesus had been arrested at night and by now it was early in the morning.

Let us once again stop for a moment to ponder over what happened here. Jesus freely gave Himself in as He was getting arrested. He did not resist for His Mission had to be fulfilled. He humbled himself like a lamb and allowed Himself to be bound by the soldiers over whom He had all the powers. And when He answered the officials of the high priest in the way He did, He was slapped by one of the officials. The official asked Him: "Is this how you answer the high priest?" In other words, the official was saying:

"Who do you think you are?" Again Jesus humbled Himself and was not provoked to retaliate. And this is where our understanding of what went on here gets limited. Once again, let us ask this question: How could the King of Kings, fully human yet fully God, with all the powers to act remain silent? How humble and how lowly could anyone be? And why could Jesus accept such humiliation? And again, the answer is just one word: Love.

The trial: Pilate washed his hands

Jesus was taken to the palace where Pilate was. There were no clear charges that the leaders brought against Him. When Pilate asked them to state the charges, they simply said that if He was not a criminal, they could not have taken Him to the palace. Pilate was not impressed. So he told them: "Take him yourselves and judge him by your own law." But, they responded: "But we have no right to execute anyone" (John 18:29-31).

In other words, they had already passed their own judgment that Jesus had to die. Pilate returned inside the palace to Jesus and asked Him whether He was the King of the Jews. This question interested Jesus who said: "Is this your own idea, or did others talk to you about me?" Pilate replied: "Am I a Jew? Your own people and chief priests handed you over to me. What is it you have done?" Jesus simply answered: "My kingdom is not of this world. If it were, my servants would fight to prevent my arrest by Jewish leaders. But now my kingdom is from another place." Pilate insisted and went on to say: "You are a king, then!" Jesus answered: "You say that I am a king. In fact, the reason I was born and came into the world is to testify to the truth. Everyone on the side of the truth listens to me" (John 18:33-37).

Pilate passed his judgment stating, "You take him and crucify him. As for me, I find no basis for charge against him" (John 19:6). But before this, Pilate's wife sent him a message saying, "Don't have anything to do with that innocent man, for I have suffered a great deal today in a dream because of him" (Mathew 27:19). The people gathered and their leaders did not accept this verdict. They wanted Jesus to die. The main reason they gave for wanting Jesus crucified was in their statement to Pilate: "We have a law, and according to that law he must die, because he claimed to be the Son of God" (John 19:7).

Now, it was the tradition that during Passover one prisoner would be released by Pilate. When he asked them if they wanted him to release Jesus or Barabbas who had taken part in an uprising, they called for the release of Barabbas and for the death of Jesus. The chief priests and the people started shouting, "Crucify him! Crucify him!" (John 19:6). Pilate took water and washed his hands when he realized that the crowd was getting rowdy. He said: "I am innocent of this man's blood, it is your responsibility" (Mathew 27:24). Pilate was reluctant to release Jesus to the priest and his officials. But, he did it saying, "Here is your king" (John 19:14).

Now, even though Jesus was found "not guilty" and was to be handed over to the priests, Pilate still ordered that Jesus be flogged by the palace soldiers who also twisted a crown of thorns and placed it on Jesus' head. Just as Jesus had told His disciples, the soldiers started to mock Him saying, "Hail, king of the Jews!" and they slapped Him in the face.

They stripped Him then put a purple robe on Him. Then they put a staff in His hand and knelt before Him as they mocked Him. They spat on Him and took the staff from His hand and struck Him with it. Finally they took off the robe and put back His clothes before they started the journey to the place of crucifixion.

Like a criminal, Jesus was taken away, yet he remained silent just as had been written by prophet Isaiah: "He was oppressed and afflicted, yet he did not open his mouth; he was led like a lamb to the slaughter, and as a sheep before its shearers is silent, so he did not open his mouth" (Isaiah 53:7). Here was Christ ready to face the most humiliating death on the cross. And I ask the question: Why? But the answer remains the same one word: Love. What a wonderful Savior!

The Testimony of Jesus

At this point, I cannot help but return to the question that I will be asking throughout this book, and I make no apologies for this:

> **"If this is how Jesus loves us – then what are we waiting for?" How is it that we are not able to love Him as He has loved us?"**

Death on the cross

Jesus was made to carry His own cross to Golgotha where He was to be crucified. I don't know about you, but as for me this was just too much humiliation and torture. For Christ to just sit back and take all these insults and abuse is beyond human understanding especially because He had all the powers with Him to refuse to accept this. But, it is this total humility that makes Jesus different from anyone else in the universe. This is the character of a lamb. It is no wonder that God hates people who are proud and haughty.

One can imagine how exhausted and tired Jesus must have been throughout this ordeal. One person called Simon was forced by the soldiers to help Jesus carry the cross. When they reached Golgotha, the soldiers offered Jesus some wine mixed with myrrh but He refused to drink it. They then went ahead a crucified Him. This was the third hour (Mark 15:25).

At the Cross

They crucified two robbers, one on each side of Jesus' cross. I don't want to imagine the kind of pain Jesus suffered as the nails were driven in His hands and feet.

And I don't want to imagine the agony and anguish that followed as He remained hanging by the tearing flesh surrounding the nails in His hands, supported by the bones of His bleeding pierced feet.

Even as Jesus agonized, people who passed by insulted and mocked Him. They said: "So! You who are going to destroy the temple and build it in three days, come down from the cross and save yourself!" (Mark 15:29). And on the cross, above Him was written in capital letters, "THIS IS THE KING OF THE JEWS." More insults.

Meanwhile, the soldiers had divided His clothes into four pieces and decided by drawing lots as to who would take the pieces. In doing this, the scriptures were fulfilled, for it was written: "They divided my garments among them and cast lots for my clothing" (Psalm 22:18; John 19:24).

As all this was happening, Mary the mother of Jesus stood watching. She was in the company of others including Mary Magdalene. One can imagine what agony Mary as a mother went through.

But she was helpless and so were the disciples and the followers of Jesus. They could only stand and watch although many of them had run away. The fulfillment of Scripture unfolded before all who witnessed the crucifixion.

The Testimony of Jesus

Jesus was crucified together with two criminals. One of them had the audacity to insult Jesus saying, "Aren't you the Christ? Save yourself and us!"

But the second criminal rebuked him saying, "Don't you fear God, since you are under the same sentence? We are punished justly, for we are getting what our deeds deserve. But this man has done nothing wrong."

And this second criminal said to Jesus, "Remember me when you come into your kingdom." And the Lord forgave him (Luke 23:40-43).

Even today, there are those who insult Jesus even in their death beds in many more ways than one. They blame God for their conditions and question God's ability to heal them. They are rebellious and often refuse to accept Jesus even when they know that their time on earth is ending. They sometimes blame their relatives, neighbors and friends and are unwilling to forgive those who may have hurt them. But the lesson from the second criminal is powerful. It shows us that it is never too late for one to accept Jesus and be forgiven.

As Jesus hang on the cross, He became thirsty. So, those around Him soaked a sponge in a jar which had vinegar and lifted it to the lips of Jesus.

After this, Jesus said, **"It is finished"** and He gave up His spirit and died. This was now the ninth hour.

At the Cross

Before He died, Jesus cried aloud: "Eloi, Eloi, lama sabachthani? Which meant, "My God, my God, why have you forsaken me? (Mark 15:33-34; John 19:30). Jesus' words of forgiveness for those who crucified Him must have echoed in the entire universe. As He hang on the cross, He said: **"Father, forgive them for they do not know what they are doing"** (Luke 23:34).This must have been a very sad moment in heaven. But all the same, the Father knew that in the end all would be well and fallen men and women would be saved.

Because the Jewish leaders did not want the crucified three to be left on the cross during the Sabbath which would start at sunset on the Preparation Day (Friday) – the day Jesus was crucified -- they requested Pilate to have their legs broken and then the bodies would be taken down. This was done to the two criminals but when they came to Jesus, they found that He was already dead. So they did not break His legs.

This was the fulfillment of scriptures for it is written that: "Not one of His bones will be broken" (Psalm 34:20; John 19:36). But one of the soldiers took a spear and pierced him on the side and there was a sudden flow of blood and water. The Master was dead.

For about three hours before Jesus died, there was darkness which started at the sixth hour until the ninth hour (Mark 15:33). The sun had stopped shining. At the ninth hour when Jesus died, the curtain of the temple was torn. The centurion who was standing in front of Jesus heard His last cry and said, "Surely, this man was the Son of God!" (Mark 15:39). At the same time the earth shook and rocks split.

It is written that the tombs broke and many of holy people who had died were raised to life (Mathew 27:51-53. As the evening approached, a certain man called Joseph of Arimathaea asked Pilate for the body of Jesus so that he could bury Him. Pilate agreed and Jesus' body was taken down. Joseph took the body, wrapped Him in some linen then placed Him in a tomb cut out of a rock. The Savior's Mission was accomplished. Jesus died as a sacrifice to atone for our sins.

The resurrection

The chief priest and the Pharisees remembered that Jesus had said that three days after His death, He will rise again. So they asked Pilate to give the orders so as to make the tomb where Jesus was buried very secure until the three days were over. For they said, "Otherwise His disciples may come and steal the body and tell the people that He has been raised from the dead.

This last deception will be worse than the first." Pilate did as he was requested. They made the tomb secure and even put a seal on it (Mathew 27:64-66).

But there was no way of keeping my Jesus in that grave, cut out by man. No stone or any number of guards could stop Him from coming out. No seal from an earthly authority could stop Him. And so He arose on the third day.

Now, this resurrection story is so sweet. Without the resurrection of Jesus, there would be no hope for mankind. The story of redemption would have ended prematurely and man would have no hope of rising from the dead to inherit the Kingdom of Heaven. But, because of Jesus and His Mission, we can now be sure that we will inherit the Kingdom. There is no other way of telling the resurrection story but to let the Bible speak to us verbatim as outlined below:

The Mathew Account: Mathew 28:1-10

In the Book of Mathew, the resurrection story is well captured. This account is written in Mathew Chapter 28 verses 1-10:

Vs 1: "After the Sabbath, at dawn on the first day of the week, Mary Magdalene and the other Mary went to look at the tomb."
Vs 2: "There was a violent earthquake, for an angel of the Lord came down from heaven and, going to the tomb, rolled back the stone and sat on it."

Vs 3: "His appearance was like lightning, and his clothes were as white as snow."

Vs 4: "The guards were so afraid of him that they shook and became like dead men."

Vs 5: "The angel said to the women, "Do not be afraid, for I know that you are looking for Jesus, who was crucified."

Vs 6: "He is not here; he has risen, just as he said. Come see the place where he lay."

Vs 7: "Then go quickly and tell his disciples: 'He has risen from the dead and is going ahead of you into Galilee. There you will see him.' Now I have told you."

The women were filled with joy, though afraid. They ran to tell the disciples. But before they reached, Jesus met them and simply said, "Greetings'. They came to Jesus' feet and worshiped Him. Then Jesus told them to go and tell the disciples to go to Galilee where they will see Him.

The Mark Account: Mark 16:1-15

This is the account of resurrection as told in the book of Mark chapter 16:

Vs 1: "When the Sabbath was over, Mary Magdalene, Mary the mother of James, and Salome brought spices so that they might go to anoint Jesus' body."

Vs 2: "Very early on the first day of the week, after sunrise, they were on their way to the tomb,"

Vs 3: "and they asked each other, 'Who will roll the stone away from the entrance of the tomb?'"

Vs 4: "But when they looked up, they saw that the stone, which was very large, had been rolled away."

Vs5: "As they entered the tomb, they saw a young man dressed in a white robe sitting on the right side, and they were alarmed."

Vs 6: "'Don't be alarmed,' he said. 'You are looking for Jesus the Nazarene, who was crucified. He has risen! He is not here. See the place where they laid him.'"

Vs 7: "But go, tell his disciples and Peter, 'He is going ahead of you into Galilee. There you will see him, just as he told you.'"

Vs 8: "Trembling and bewildered, the women went out and fled from the tomb. They said nothing because they were afraid."

The Luke Account: Luke 24:1-8

And Luke the doctor wrote about the resurrection in the book of Luke chapter 24:

The Testimony of Jesus

Vs 1: "On the first day of the week, very early in the morning, the women took spices they had prepared and went to the tomb."

Vs 2: They found the stone rolled away from the tomb,"

Vs 3: "but when they entered, they did not find the body of the Lord Jesus."

Vs 4: "While they were wondering about this, suddenly two men in clothes that gleamed like lightning stood beside them."

Vs 5: "In their fright the women bowed down with their faces to the ground, but the men said to them, 'Why do you look for the living among the dead?'"

Vs 6: "He is not here; he has arisen! Remember how he told you, while he was still with you in Galilee:

Vs 7: 'The Son of man must be delivered over to the hands of sinners, be crucified and on the third day be raised again.'"

Thus, after His resurrection, Jesus first appeared to the women who went to anoint Him. In the book of John, it is written that Mary Magdalene who was among the first to see Jesus could not recognize Him at first. She even thought Jesus was a gardener.

But Jesus called her by her name and immediately she realized it was Him. She cried out in Aramaic, "Rabboni" (which means "Teacher"). Then Jesus told her, "Do not touch me, for I have not yet ascended to the Father. Go instead to my brothers and tell them, 'I am ascending to my Father and your Father, to my God and your God'" (John 20:15-17).

The women went and told the disciples what they had witnessed. At first, the disciples did not believe what they were being told. Peter even ran to the tomb to ascertain for himself what the women were saying.

Then Jesus finally appeared to His disciples in Galilee. The first thing He said was, "Peace be with you" (Luke 24:36). They were very frightened thinking that they had seen a ghost. But Jesus went on to say, "Why are you troubled, and why do doubts arise in your minds? Look at my hands and my feet. It is I myself! Touch me and see; a ghost does not have flesh and bones, as you see I have" (Luke 24:38-39).

And given that they still did not believe, He showed them His hands and feet and then asked for something to eat. They gave Him broiled fish and He ate it in their presence.

The disciples told Thomas that they had seen the Lord. It seems that Thomas was not with them when Jesus appeared to them.

But Thomas said, "Unless I see nail marks in his hands and put my finger where the nails were, and put my hand on his side, I will not believe it" (John 20:25). Then Jesus suddenly stood by them and said, "Peace be with you!" He then specifically addressed Thomas who had doubted when he was told that Jesus had risen. Jesus told him: "Put your finger here; see my hands. Reach out and put it into my side. Stop doubting and believe." This is when Thomas responded, "My Lord and my God." Jesus answered him saying, "Because you have seen me, you have believed; blessed are those who have not seen and yet have believed" (John 20:26-29).

End of the Mission

The prophecy was fulfilled. Jesus was born, revealed Himself and God the Father to us, showed His love and compassion, performed many miracles and taught us. But He was rejected, tortured, mocked, spat on, crucified and buried. Yet He arose on the third day as He promised. He overcame trials and tribulations just to save the lost. He endured the humiliation, the cross and ultimately the grave as he suffered severe separation from the Father. As Jesus arose, there must have been joy in heaven. And the human race was finally saved. The Mission finally came to an end. The Master arose. He died on a Friday, rested in the grave on the Sabbath day and arose on a Sunday.

At the Cross

Jesus now had to return to the Father. He had appeared to the disciples over a period of forty days after the resurrection. And just as He started His Mission, He spoke to them again about the Kingdom of Heaven (Acts 1:3). As He was about to ascend, Jesus said to His disciples: "This is what is written: The Christ will suffer and rise from the dead on the third day, and repentance and forgiveness of sins will be preached in his name to all nations, beginning at Jerusalem. You are the witnesses of these things. I am going to send you what my Father has promised; but stay in the city until you have been clothed with power from on high" (Luke 24:46-49).

Jesus then led His disciples to a place near Bethany where He lifted His hands and blessed the disciples. As He was blessing them, He was taken up and ascended into heaven. The good shepherd who laid His life for His sheep went to the Father to start the next phase of getting the lost sheep back home. We do not know the time or the hour, but let us all be ready.

Jesus, our intercessor and High Priest in the Heavenly Sanctuary will surely return to take us home. He will surely return to rescue us from the dragon who was hurled down to the earth and is now busy making war against the elect – those who obey God's commandments and hold on to the testimony of Jesus (Revelation 12:17). It is this testimony that this book is all about.

CHAPTER 10

IN THE FOOTSTEPS OF JESUS

"If any of you would come after me, he must deny himself and take up his cross and follow me." Mathew 16:24

The clarion call that Jesus has made to all mankind is: "REPENT, FOR THE KINGDOM OF HEAVEN IS NEAR" and then He adds, "FOLLOW ME". Yes, all of us must wake up and follow Him into the kingdom.

Jesus came into the world as was prophesied in the scriptures. He came to bring back the lost into the Kingdom of Heaven. And He came in a humble manner being born in a manger. When, in His humanly form, He attained the age of thirty years he began to preach the Kingdom of Heaven. He taught His disciples and us in a simple, effective and most powerful way.

Although He knew everything from the beginning into eternity and could have revealed all that was in Him, He chose to be humble and to use simple language in parables and stories which anyone could enjoy listening to, understand and remember.

Jesus the Way showed us the How. In addition to using simple language and stories, He also used simple people, the fishermen, the tax collectors and sinners to spread His message. But, many today have failed to learn from the

Savior. For, we have become more knowledgeable with PhDs and are often quick to show our style and knowledge of scriptures, making everything very complicated. At the end of an exegesis, speakers often wait for applause before they continue with their message.

Yes, exegesis. I have used this word to demonstrate how complex we have become. Exegesis simply means "explanation or interpretation of a text, a Bible text." And in addition to this complexity, the "fishermen", the "tax collectors" and sinners have all been made to become passive listeners and observers.

We are the fishermen and the sinners who have also on our own decided to be observers because we are convinced that without the "exegetic ability and knowledge" we may not be effective in spreading the message of the Kingdom of Heaven. Many of us believe that after going to the places of worship and returning tithes, all will be well in so far as our journey to heaven is concerned. Let us remember, however, that the message has been made simple by Jesus. All that is left for us is to follow His example.

And let us believe that we are called to be part of the Great Commission to take the message of hope about the second coming of Christ and of the Kingdom of Heaven to the ends of the earth and to make disciples of all nations. When we trust in God, the Holy Spirit will lead us into the whole truth and show us the way. Jesus said, "It is written in the Prophets: 'They will all be taught by God.' Everyone who has heard the Father and learnt from Him comes to me" (John 6:45).

Jesus preached the word, but he also healed the sick and gave food to the hungry and gave us hope in His second coming. In doing this, He showed compassion to all. Today, many religious institutions, individual evangelists and Christians preach the Word but do not care for the sick, the poor, the hungry, the widows and the orphans. In fact, many of us ran away from the perceived "sinners" and destitutes. Thus, we show little compassion to the less fortunate in the society.

Well, let us follow in the footsteps of Jesus and practice what He taught has us. Jesus chose His disciples from simple and ordinary people. His first disciples were Simon and his brother Andrew both of whom were fishermen. Jesus said to them, "Come, follow me, and I will make you fishers of men" (Mark 1:17). At once, the two left their fishing nets and followed Jesus. Yes, they became fishers of men, bringing souls to Christ. Then Jesus found James son of Zebedee and John his brother. These two were also fishermen. Just like Simon and Andrew, they also left their nets without delay and followed Jesus. The other eight disciples were: Mathew (a tax collector), Philip, Thomas, James son of Alphaeus, Thaddaeus, Simon the Zealot, Bartholomew and Judas Iscariot.

In the Footsteps of Jesus

When Jesus sent out His disciples, He gave them authority to drive out demons and heal every disease and sickness (Mathew 10:1). In His own words, He said to them: "Heal the sick, raise the dead, cleanse those who have leprosy, drive out demons. Freely you have received; freely give" (Mathew 10:8).

We have not been given authority to raise the dead. But every gift we have received from the Lord has been given freely and freely we should use these gifts to spread the word of God and also reach out to the needy. And it is written: **"Now to each one the manifestation of the spirit is given for the common good."** (1st Corinthians 12:7).

Those who have been blessed by various gifts should use them for the common good and not just for private gain. Therefore, as we spread the word of God, let us not neglect the compassionate actions that Jesus taught His disciples and us to do.

In dealing with the sick, for example, we may not have healing powers, but Christ has given us knowledge that has led to the discovery of drugs and medicines which were not there at the time He spoke to His disciples. So today, we have ability to help those who are sick and are unable to access care. In addition to caring for them, we also need to pray with them and console them and ask Christ to heal them.

We should also have the compassion to share the little we have with the poor and the destitute. It may be just giving away a dress or a shirt to a needy person or sharing the little food we have with the hungry. In particular, we should look out for widows and orphans. And we should make it our mission to visit those in prisons and show love to them. So, there is much that Christians can do and accomplish as we follow in the footsteps of Jesus. There is no one on earth with hands, ears, eyes and feet who cannot help another human being. Even the deaf and the dumb as well as the blind have much to give to the society.

It is written that, "Religion that God our Father accepts as pure and faultless is this: to look after orphans and widows in their distress and to keep oneself from being polluted by the world" (James 1:27).

In order to make disciples of all nations, we must also go to the unreached people who in the days past were called Gentiles. Paul was himself chosen by Christ to take the word to the Gentiles. One day he went to the high priest in Jerusalem and asked to be given letters to synagogues in Damascus so that anyone found to belong to the Way, the followers of Jesus, would be taken prisoners. He got his letters and was on his way.

However, as he approached Damascus, he suddenly saw light from heaven that flashed around him. He fell down and he heard a voice saying, "Saul, Saul, why do you persecute me?" Saul asked, "Who are you, Lord?" Then he heard the voice saying, "I am Jesus, whom you are persecuting." Jesus then told him to go into the city of Damascus and he would be told what to do. He became blind and was led into the city (Acts 9:1-9).

As all this was happening to Paul, Jesus appeared in a vision to a disciple called Ananias who was in Damascus. Jesus told Ananias this: "Go into the house of Judas on the Straight Street and ask for a man from Tarsus named Saul, for he is praying. In a vision he has seen a man named Ananias come and place his hands on him to restore his sight" (Acts 9:10-11).

Ananias was afraid of Saul for he knew of how Saul had persecuted the followers of Christ. But Jesus told him, "Go! This man is my chosen instrument to proclaim my name to the Gentiles and their kings and to the people of Israel. I will show him how much he must suffer for my name" (Acts 9:15).

Just like Saul whose name was changed to Paul was chosen, so are many of us today. But we are reluctant and need someone to open our eyes so that we can see the potential in each one of us to proclaim the good news to all around us and beyond. And that someone is Jesus who opened the eyes of Paul. Jesus is waiting and standing at the door. But we are refusing to open our hearts saying that "we can only do it if Jesus is in us", yet Jesus has said that He is willing and is standing at the door. As we have already stated in this book, the problem is on our side and not on Jesus' side. We are the ones who have refused to open that door for Jesus to come in and eat with us.

In this chapter, we will focus on one clarion call made by Jesus and that is: "Take up your cross and follow me." By carrying His cross to Calvary and surrendering His will to the Father, Jesus has showed us the way. Let us read on.

Take up your cross and follow me

Jesus carried His cross. The burden He had was the sin that was heaped upon Him by fallen human beings. But He went all the way and died for us in order to atone for our sins. So when He calls upon us to take up our cross and follow Him, He is saying to us that we must carry whatever burdens we may have, suffer for Him and make sacrifices in our lives so as to become His true followers. And, He says that we must deny ourselves, take up our cross and follow Him.

Jesus told His disciples in Mathew 10:37-39 that:

> "Anyone who loves his father or mother more than me is not worthy of me; anyone who loves his son or daughter more than me is not worthy of me; and **anyone who does not take his cross and follow me is not worthy of me**. Whoever finds his life will lose it and whoever loses his life for my sake will find it."

The Holy Spirit has led me to list twelve things we need to pay attention to as each one carries his or her cross to follow Jesus.

1. We should be ready to die for what we believe in
Nearly all of us are afraid of dying. This is natural. But when we are called to take a stand for Jesus and face tribulations and even persecutions, would we still be afraid to face any consequences, even death? The answer is obvious for it is inevitable that many of us will be afraid and may not stand the test.

Even Peter failed the test when Jesus was arrested. But in the end, he was able to stand the test as he was crucified upside down for believing in Jesus. Stephen is another good example of one who was ready to die for Jesus. And he was stoned to death for believing in Him.

So the question each one of us should answer is: "Am I ready to die for Jesus?"

One may not have to be physically dead, but the least that is expected of a true follower of Christ is to believe and surrender to Him and to have total commitment and faith in Him to the point where we live our lives daily for Him. We need to love the Lord our God as He has loved us. This we must do by following Him with all our hearts, mind and soul and at all cost, even if it means our physical death. For death on earth is only but sleep. We believe that those who die in Christ will inherit the Kingdom of Heaven.

Therefore, Christians should aim to grow to the highest level of spiritual growth and to the point where death on earth, after one has surrendered to Christ, should be seen as simple sleep and not a problem.

Jesus told His disciples: "Whoever wants to be my disciple must deny himself and take up their cross and follow me. For whoever wants to save his life will lose it, but whoever loses their life for me will find it. What good will it be for someone to gain the whole world, yet forfeit their soul? Or what can anyone give in exchange for their soul?" (Mathew 16:24-26).

And in the book of Mark the same message by Christ is written: "Whoever wants to be my disciple must deny themselves and take up their cross and follow me. For whoever wants to save their life will lose it, but whoever loses their life for me and for the gospel will save it" (Mark 8:34-35).

Christ knew that His disciples will lose their lives because of Him. And today this still remains the case. True followers of Christ must be ready to die for Him. This we do to glory the Father. Now, if one takes a closer look at the trends in the world today, we can see that more and more; the world is rejecting Christ. The bad has become the good. The lie has become the truth for many as they say that truth is "relative" depending on the circumstances around which the truth is being seen. Well, I have bad news for all of us:

In the Footsteps of Jesus

Truth is always the truth and it does not change. And it is likely that true followers of Christ will face persecutions in this world where the truth is being more and more rejected. Now if this happens, will you and I be left standing? The answer must be yes for those who have decided to take up their cross and follow Jesus. But for those who say no, there is more soul searching to be done. As a matter of fact, persecution is already here to be faced by Christians. The only problem is that we Christians are not ready to stand up for Christ and face persecution. For example, if we stood up strongly against authorities who reject God outright, we would obviously be thrown in jail or even be killed.

Remember the words written by John the Revelator in Revelation 12:10-11: "Then I heard a loud voice in heaven say: 'Now have come the salvation and the power and the kingdom of our God, and the authority of his Jesus. For the accuser of our brothers and sisters, who accuses them before our God day and night, has been hurled down. They overcame him by the blood of the Lamb and by the word of their testimony; they did not love their lives so much as to shrink from death."

And yes, let us remember Shadrach, Meshach and Abednego who refused to worship the image of gold that King Nebuchadnezzar had made and had decreed that everyone must fall down and worship. They did not love their loves so much as to shrink from death. The three

Hebrew boys were not intimidated by the authority of the king and the threat to have them thrown into a hot furnace.

King Nebuchadnezzar asked the three, "Is it true, Shadrach, Meshach and Abednego, that you do not serve my gods or worship the image of gold I have set up?" (Daniel 3:14). He then went on to tell them to worship the image or face the blazing furnace. But the three responded:

> "King Nebuchadnezzar, we do not need to defend ourselves before you in this matter. If we are thrown into the blazing furnace, the God we serve is able to deliver us from it, and he will deliver us from Your Majesty's hand. But even if he does not, we want you to know, Your Majesty, that we will not serve your gods or worship the image of gold you have set up" (Daniel 3:16-18).

The king was furious and ordered the furnace to be heated seven times hotter. You may recall that during this era, no one dared talk back to or argue with any king. The three were certainly strong and courageous. They knew who they believed in. The Lord our God, the Almighty was with them. So when they were thrown into the furnace the king was surprised to see a fourth person walking freely in the fire with the three while the soldiers who threw them into the furnace were burned up. Shadrach, Meshach and Abednego stood for the Lord. They came out alive and victorious. But it did not matter to them whether or not they were going to die. This is what Jesus is calling us to do as we take up our cross and follow Him. We must trust in the Lord our God. The Apostle Paul summarized the need for total commitment to Christ when he said, "Here is a trustworthy saying: If we died with him, we will also live with him; if we endure, we will also reign with him. If we disown him, he will also disown us; if we are faithless, he remains faithful, for he cannot disown himself" (2 Timothy 2:11-13).

What a wonderful Savior!

And Paul also said that our light and momentary troubles are achieving for us an eternal glory that outweighs our struggles. He said: "We are pressed on every side, but not crushed, perplexed, but not in despair; persecuted, but not abandoned; struck down, but not destroyed. We always carry around in our body the death of Jesus, so that the life of Jesus may also be revealed in our body" (2nd Corinthians 4:8-10). Jesus said that blessed are those who are persecuted because of righteousness, for theirs is the Kingdom of Heaven (Mathew 5:10).

2. Surrender your will to Christ

As it is written, God the Father has placed all things under Christ. This includes you and I. So, just as Christ surrendered His will to the Father, we have been called to surrender our will to Christ who takes care of us to the glory of the Father. In the book of Colossians chapter 3 verse 3, it is written: "For you died, and your life is now hidden with Christ in God." Yes, we should be dead to self and alive in Christ.

Jesus gave us the best example as He surrendered His will to the Father. This was demonstrated when one day Jesus went with His disciples to the garden of Gethsemane. He went with Peter, John and James and was sorrowful as he told them: "My soul is overwhelmed with sorrow to the point of death. Stay here and keep watch with me."

After he had gone a little distance from them, He fell face down to the ground and began to pray saying, "My Father, if it is possible, may this cup be taken from me. Yet not as I will, but as you will." We do not know how the Father responded, but Jesus went on to pray and He said, "My Father, if it is not possible for this cup to be taken away unless I drink it, may your will be done" (Mathew 26:36-42).

Similarly, as we follow Jesus we have to surrender our will to God and let the Holy Spirit lead us. **The highest place we should be is the feet of Jesus**. If we find ourselves to be taller than the height of the foot of Christ then we need prayers. We must humble ourselves to death and prepare to suffer loss for a greater gain, for there is much treasure in loss as we search for the Kingdom of Heaven. We need to surrender because all the work we do, the words we speak, the thoughts that build, the strength and health to accomplish anything, and the time and space available to do anything, all come from God – freely given.

It is written: "And we know that in all things God works for the good of those who love him, who have been called according to his purpose" (Romans 8:28).

Therefore, there is nothing that will happen to us that is not a blessing. We should not be afraid even if we face tribulations. If we open the doors of our hearts to Christ, we will find it easy to surrender since everything is in the hands of the Lord and there is nothing we can do on our own.

We must learn to humble ourselves before the Lord for He hates proud and haughty people. It is written: "Humble yourselves, therefore, under God's mighty hand, that he may lift you up in due time. Cast all your anxiety on him because he cares for you" (1 Peter 5:6-7).

3. Play by the rules

As we surrender, we have to play by the rules. Jesus said, "If you love me keep my commands" (John 14:14). Those who surrender their will must play according to the command of whoever they have surrendered to. The Lord has given us the commandments to follow. And Jesus gave us an example by keeping all the commandments including the Fourth Commandment on the Sabbath. If we open the doors of our hearts for Him to come in, He will cause us to follow these commandments and be obedient to the Lord Almighty. We need to remember that we are soldiers of the cross. And as soldiers, we are bound by the commands of the captain or the commander. In this case, Jesus is our captain.

And as Paul has written, "No one serving as a soldier gets involved in civilian affairs – he wants to please his commanding officer. Similarly, if anyone competes as an athlete, he does not receive the victor's crown unless he competes according to the rules" (2nd Timothy 2:4-5). By breaking the Commandments of God we are involving ourselves in "civilian affairs."

And by breaking the rules of a race as athletes on a journey to inherit the Kingdom of Heaven, we may be disqualified from receiving the crown. There are many examples in the Bible of those who surrendered their lives to God. They came to God as they were. And they were willing and ready to serve the Lord. Job, Daniel, Elijah, Elisha, Jeremiah, Isaiah, Samuel, Joseph, Ruth, Peter, Paul, John, and David were among them.

Yes, David was one solid example. He loved the Lord. But he was not without sin. What must have pleased God about David was his love for the Lord that led to confession of his sins and search for forgiveness. And God said, "I have found David son of Jesse a man after my own heart; he will do everything I want him to do" (Acts 13:22).

There is need for us to learn from David and surrender as we set our hearts to love the Lord and all mankind. Jesus said, "My command is this: Love each other as I have loved you. Greater love has no-one than this, that he lay down his life for his friends. You are my friends if you do what I command" (John 15:12-14). Therefore, let us love the Lord and surrender completely as we take up our cross to follow Jesus.

4. Give up something good

The third consideration we must have as we prepare to take up our cross and follow Jesus is that we must be ready to give up something good; something that is dear to our hearts. Jesus set the highest example when He gave up His heavenly seat at the right hand of the Father to come down, suffer and carry the cross on which He was crucified for our sins. He was crucified, yet He was innocent.

Yes, we must deny ourselves the good things so that we can get something better which is the Kingdom of Heaven. For many of us, the world offers many pleasures that satisfy the flesh. We love our jobs and we love our properties.

This is human and there is nothing wrong with this. But if our jobs and our possessions take us away from Christ then it is better for us to reconsider our position. We need to give up our comfort zones and step out to work for the Lord including helping the needy. In doing this, we should give of our best. There are many times when someone in need may approach us asking for help and we often end up giving what we do not need, for example the clothes we would like to throw away and the food we do not want.

Well, we need to re-examine ourselves because those who carry the cross must give of their best.

As it is written, "Do not withhold good from those to whom it is due, when it is in the power of your hand to do so. Do not say to your neighbor, 'Go, and come back, and tomorrow I will give it, when you have it with you" (Proverbs 3:27-28, NKJV).

The Apostle Peter says, "Each of you should use whatever gift you have received to serve others, as faithful stewards of God's grace in its various forms" (1 Peter 4:10). And as we give to the needy, let us remember the words of Jesus when he said, "So when you give to the needy, do not announce it with trumpets, as the hypocrites do in the synagogues and on the streets, to be honored by others.

Truly I tell you, they have received their reward in full. But when you give to the needy, do not let your left hand know what your right hand is doing, so that your giving may be secret. Then your Father, who sees what is done in secret, will reward you" (Mathew 6:2-4).

And then there is the work of the Lord that we must be a part of. Jesus said that the message of the Kingdom of Heaven will be preached to the ends of the earth and then the end will come. He also commissioned us saying: "Therefore go and make disciples of all nations, baptizing them in the name of Father and of the Son and of the Holy Spirit, and teaching them to obey everything I have commanded you. And surely I am with you always, to the very end of the age" (Mathew 28:19-20).

Now is the time when the followers of Christ must sacrifice to the Lord and contribute significantly towards getting the message out to those who are yet to know Jesus. And these unreached places may be just within our neighborhoods. Let us reach out with God's word and with compassion as Jesus did. We should remember that we have been blessed so that we can be a blessing to others. And let us not forget that "it is more blessed to give than to receive" (Acts 20:35).

5. Pray all the time

The cross can be heavy. It was heavy for Christ and I am sure it can be even heavier for us. Throughout His Mission, Jesus stayed connected with His Father. Jesus prayed all the time and often retreated to lonely places to be alone with the Father.

If Jesus Himself needed this much connection with the Father, then how much more connected with the Father and with our Lord Jesus Christ should we be if we are to carry our cross? It is inevitable that we need to be on our knees praying and asking for the strength and courage to carry on. We need to pray for protection against the evil one as we journey towards the prize that is in Christ Jesus.

We need to pray unceasingly and with faith. And we need to declare a fast from time to time as we dedicate ourselves reverently to the Lord in prayer. As we do so, we need to have faith and to believe. Jesus said, "Ask and it will be given to you; seek and you will find; knock and the door will be opened to you. For everyone who asks receives; he who seeks finds; and to him who knocks, the door will be opened" Mathew 7:7-8).

Yes, Let us pray as if we have already received. Let us commit ourselves to the Lord as we pray, for it is written: "For the eyes of the Lord range throughout the earth to strengthen those whose hearts are fully committed to him" (2nd Chronicles 16:13). Let us trust in the Lord for we are His children.

There is also need for us to pray for one another because intercessory prayers are powerful. The Apostle James writes: "Is any one of you in trouble? He should pray. Is anyone happy? Let him sing songs of praise. Is any one of you sick? He should call the elders of the church to pray over him and anoint him with oil in the name of the Lord. And the prayer offered in faith will make a sick person well; the Lord will raise him up. If he has sinned, he will be forgiven." James added that the prayer of a righteous man is powerful and effective (James 5:14-15).

As it is written, let us "rejoice always, pray continually, and give thanks in all circumstances; for this is God's will for you in Christ Jesus" (1st Thessalonians 5:16-18). And let us pray in spirit and in truth for it is written: "Yet a time is coming and has now come when the true worshippers will worship the Father in spirit and truth, for these are the kind of worshipers the Father seeks. God is spirit, and his worshipers must worship in spirit and in truth" (John 4:23-24).

6. Be ready to encounter thorns on the way and to be spat on

As one carries the cross, one will encounter problems or thorns on the way. And this is experienced by many including those who have dedicated their lives to Jesus. Jesus faced many tribulations on the way and was even crowned with a crown of thorns, so we who are His followers will also meet thorns on the way. Many Christians have fallen on the wayside because of the afflictions and temptations they come across.

There are many communities where people, even Christians, often turn to other earthly ways including witchcraft in search of healing. There are also those who, through no fault of their own, end up in dysfunctional relationships and suffer pain and anguish sometimes because of their beliefs. Well, whatever affliction or pain we have, let us stay the course and carry that cross for Jesus. And whenever we experience such circumstances, let us remember these words of David: "God is our refuge and strength, an ever-present help in trouble" (Psalm 46:1). Apostle Paul talked about a thorn in his flesh that tormented him. Although we do not know the nature of this thorn, it is obvious that it was hurting him because he said that three times he asked the Lord to take it away but the Lord did not answer his prayer simply telling Paul that "My grace is sufficient for you, for my power is made perfect in weakness" (2nd Corinthians 12:9).

Paul said that because of this assurance, he would boast more about his weaknesses. He said, "That is why, for Christ's sake, I delight in weaknesses, insults, in hardships, in persecutions, in difficulties. For when I am weak, then I am strong" (2nd Corinthians 12:10).

So the thorns we meet on our way should strengthen us and not weaken us. Further, as we come to Jesus, our friends may reject us or even mock us. Our families may also reject us and behave as if they are actually "spitting" on us because of our belief in Jesus. These will be among the thorns we must be prepared to encounter. Our comfort should be Jesus who went through this experience but did not open His mouth. Through His blood we have become victorious. The Lord says, "They will fight against you but will not overcome you, for I am with you and will rescue you" (Jeremiah 1:19).

We need to know that even in the worship houses there are thorns. The Apostle Paul wrote, "I urge you brothers and sisters, to watch out for those who cause divisions and put obstacles in your way that are contrary to the teaching you have received. Keep away from them. For such people are not serving our Lord Christ, but their own appetites. By smooth talk and flattery they deceive the minds of the naïve people" (Romans 16: 17-18).

Paul may not have been talking to people in any given church, but his advice is relevant to all. Let us not be among those who become thorns in the lives of fellow believers and even of unbelievers who need to be welcomed into the fold. Let us encourage one another to keep our eyes fixed on Jesus and not on our pastors, elders and members of our congregations.

7. Do not expect any help

The Lord is always watching to see that His word is fulfilled (Jeremiah 1:12). And He has told us to be brave and to have courage. So with Him on our side, we are safe and need no help from anyone else. With God on our side we will be able to carry that cross to the finish line. One of my

The Testimony of Jesus

most favorable verses in the Bible is Romans 8:28 that says, "And we know that in all things God works for the good of those who love Him, who have been called according to His good purpose." This is so true. Even when no one is there to help us carry our cross, it is good for us to just bear our burdens without fear. For, our unseen helper and friend is always on our side. And those who suffer more become stronger in the Lord.

Jesus carried His cross alone. He was prepared for it and really needed no help. The soldiers, who were leading Him to Calvary, however forced one called Simon from Cyrene to help Jesus carry the cross.

Everybody else watched and some were even overjoyed to see Jesus suffer. But the Lord was going all the way with His cross. He had chosen to go to Golgotha and no obstacle could stop Him from bringing redemption to the lost. Similarly, as we take up our cross to follow Jesus, the same may happen to us. Each of us should be prepared to carry the cross alone. We should take responsibility for our actions and not blame others for our predicaments. But as we do, we should know that Jesus is there for us and will make our burdens light for we can do all things through Christ who gives us strength (Philippians 4:13).

So, even when we may think that we are alone in our struggles, we should remember that we have an unseen friend who is always there for us.

8. All your friends will run away

As one takes up his or her cross to follow Jesus, one's friends may abandon them. This may be due to the changes that may occur in the behavior of the one who has become a believer.

Even ones' family may be hostile. A good example is what happened to Jesus when one day He entered a house and, as was always the case whenever people knew He was around, a crowd came to Him. So Jesus and His disciples were so busy with the crowd that they were not even able to eat.

When Jesus' family heard about this, they were not happy and wanted to take care of Him. In fact, they said, "He is out of His mind." And the teachers of the law also added their pitch to this saying that Jesus was possessed by demons (Mark 3:20-22).

So here we see that even the family of Jesus thought He was out of His mind. In a way, they were misjudging Him and rejecting what He was doing.

Similarly, our families and friends may say that we are out of our minds when get to know Jesus deeply, but this should not deter us. All we are asked to do is to forgive them and simply pray for them so that they may also see the light and seek the Kingdom of Heaven. Apart from our families and friends, we may also be rejected by our communities as was the case with Jesus who was rejected in

His own hometown in Nazareth. This became evident when one day He went to teach in the synagogue in His hometown. Those who heard Him said:

"Where did this man get these things? What's this wisdom that has been given Him? What are these remarkable miracles he is performing? Isn't this the carpenter? Isn't this Mary's son and brother of James, Joseph, Judas and Simon? Aren't his sisters here with us?" Jesus simply said to them, "A prophet is not without honor except in his own town, among his relatives and in his own home."

Jesus was surprised at the lack of their faith and decided not to do any miracles there (Mark 6:1-6). And we all know what happened to the disciples of Jesus on the night He was arrested.

They all run away and denied ever knowing Him.
Therefore, let us be prepared to leave old friends as we walk with Jesus. In any case, we may make new friends who also believe in Jesus. But even if we don't, Jesus is enough as a friend.

If we find Jesus, we will automatically find that we will have a tendency to turn away from the many pleasures of this world. This we must do because if we keep looking back like Lot's wife, we may begin to backtrack and may weaken our relationship and friendship with our Lord and Savior.

9. Give glory to God and do not expect praise from anyone

In everything we do, all glory and honor must be to the Lord Almighty. This is how a follower of Christ should be. We need to walk humbly with the Lord. We should not expect or wait for praise from anyone for everything we do must be to glorify our Father in heaven. In any case, even if we expected praise, it will most likely not be given to us.

The people we serve will wait for the smallest mistake we make and pounce on it to get to us. They will not remember any good you may have done to them. The people you help may also be the ones who accuse you of wrong doing even if there is nothing wrong you have done to them.

And if you help anyone, encourage them not to broadcast the help you have given to them to their friends or families. Jesus healed many people and He encouraged them not to tell anyone how they got healed. For example, Jesus healed a man with leprosy then told him, "See that you don't tell anyone. But go and show yourself to the priest and offer the gift Moses commanded, as a testimony to them" (Mathew 8:4).

Remember also that as we work in the Lord's vineyard, we may be ridiculed and scorned for doing the right things instead of receiving praise. This was evident when Jesus called Mathew the tax collector: He went with him to his

The Testimony of Jesus

house to have dinner. The Pharisees saw Him and asked His disciples, "Why does your teacher eat with tax collectors and sinners?" When Jesus heard this, He told them that He did not come to call the righteous but sinners. Let us pray for those who judge us wrongly and also pray that we do not do the same to them. We, the soldiers of the cross, must carry our cross sacrificially and with joy in our hearts as we look forward to the second coming of Jesus. We must forget any praise on earth because the only praise that matters is the one we will get when we are received by the Lord in His Kingdom.

Also, we need not think highly of ourselves and in so doing praising ourselves. Remember the words of Paul when he was taking about righteousness: "Brothers and sisters, I do not consider myself yet to have taken hold of it. But, one thing I do: Forgetting what is behind and straining toward what is ahead, I press on toward the goal to win the prize for which God has called me heavenward in Christ Jesus" (Philippians 3:13-14).

Further, we should not forget that "whatever we do, whether in word or deed, we do it all in the name of Jesus, giving thanks to God the Father through Him" (Colossians 3:17). And in the book of Isaiah, it is written: "Lord, you establish peace for us; all that we have accomplished you have done for us" (Isaiah 26:12). If the Lord has done everything for us, then there is nothing left for which we should seek approval or praise. Apostle Paul also wrote: "May I never boast of anything except in the cross of our Lord Jesus Christ, through which the world has been crucified to me, and I to the world" (Galatians 6:14). Yes, we must give glory to God in everything we do.

One of the worst occasions when someone denied God His glory was when Moses was asked by the Lord to speak to a rock so that the children of Israel who had come out of Egypt would see God's glory.

The whole Israel community arrived at a place called Kadesh in the desert of Zin. They had no water and started to complain and quarrel with Moses saying, "If only we had died when our brothers fell dead before the Lord. Why did you bring the Lord's community into this wilderness, that we and our stock should die here? Why did you bring us out of Egypt to this terrible place? It has no grain or figs, grapevines or pomegranates. And there is no water to drink?" (Number 20:3-5).

The Lord showed compassion on the children of Israel and told Moses and Aaron to gather them and asked Moses to speak to a rock before their eyes so that they will see the glory of God as water pours out of the rock. Moses gathered the Israelites and said to them: **"Listen, you rebels, must we bring you water out of this rock?"** (Numbers 20:10). Now, look at Moses. Instead of giving God full glory, he decided to take a share of it when he said, "must WE bring you water out of this rock." This did not please the Lord. To make matters worse, Moses then went ahead and struck the rock with his rod instead of speaking to it as the Lord had told him.

The children of Israel had seen Moses use the rod to do miracles. So for Moses, this might have been another opportunity to "show them" what he could do. The Lord was not amused for He said to Moses and Aaron: "Because you did not trust in me enough to honor me as holy in the sight of Israelites, you will not bring this community to the land I give them" (Numbers 20:12).

Thus, Moses was punished. But we know that in the end, Moses was very obedient unto the Lord as God instructed him to climb Mount Nebo where he died (Deuteronomy 34:1-5). We, who have been called the children of God, should remain faithful and obedient unto the Lord, giving Him glory and honor in each and every situation.

10. Forgive everyone

Forgiveness is the key to the Kingdom of Heaven. For, if our Father did not forgive mankind through the sacrifice and death of Christ, we would all be locked out of the Kingdom of Heaven. One of the most powerful stories of forgiveness came from Joseph who forgave his brothers after he was sold to the Ishmaelites and taken to Egypt. He was blessed to occupy a high position in Pharaoh's palace and had the opportunity to bring his brothers and their father to Egypt when there was no food in their motherland. When his father, Jacob, died in Egypt and his remains were taken to be buried, as he had willed, in the land of his ancestors in Canaan, Joseph, his brothers and Pharaoh's officials went to witness the burial.

As Joseph and his brothers returned to Egypt following the burial, the brothers became afraid and wondered whether or not Joseph would revenge upon them after the death of their father. They sent this message to Joseph: "Your father left these instructions before he died: 'This is what you are to say to Joseph: I ask you to forgive your brothers the sins and the wrongs they committed in treating you so badly.' Now please forgive the sins of the servants of the God of your father" (Genesis 50:17).

When Joseph received this message, he wept. He said to his brothers, "Don't be afraid. Am I in the place of God? You intended to harm me, but God intended it for good to accomplish what is now being done, saving of many lives. So then, don't be afraid. I will provide for you and your children" (Genesis 50:19-21).

This was forgiveness at work. But wait. Let us take a look at the greatest forgiveness that came at the cross. Jesus had been persecuted, mocked, spat on and abused. And as He was hanging on the cross dying, He said, "Father, forgive them, for they do not know what they are doing" (Luke 23:34).

The Testimony of Jesus

Yes, we were forgiven. Jesus atoned for all our sins. During His teachings, Jesus taught us how to pray and how to forgive.

And he asked us to pray to the Father and to say this: "Forgive us our debts, as we also have forgiven our debtors" (Mathew 6:12).

I wonder how many of us know what we are saying as we say the Lord's Prayer. Do we know that we are taking a stand as we tell God in prayer to forgive us as we have already forgiven all those who wrong us?

Once again let us remember what Jesus told Peter when he asked, "Lord how many times shall I forgive my brother or sister who sins against me? Up to seven times?" Jesus answered Peter: "I tell you, not seven times, but seventy-seven times" (Mathew 18:21-22).

Further, the Apostle Paul said this in the book of Colossians 3:12-14: "Therefore, as God's chosen people, holy and dearly loved, clothe yourselves with compassion, kindness, humility, gentleness and patience. Bear with each other and forgive whatever grievances you may have against one another.

Forgive as the Lord forgave you. And over all these virtues put on love, which binds them together in perfect unity." Therefore, as we carry that cross we must forgive and forgive up to seventy times seven. In doing this, we shall show love and will give glory to our Father in heaven.

11. Have faith

We must be strong and courageous and have faith in Christ and believe in Him. This is the faith that the friends of the paralytic who overcame all obstacles to find Jesus had. They tore the roof of a house where Jesus was and lowered their paralytic friend down to Jesus. This was in Capernaum.

When Jesus saw their faith he told the paralytic this, "Son, your sins are forgiven" (Mark 2:5). But when the teachers of the law heard this, they said to themselves, "Why does this fellow talk like that? He is blaspheming! Who can forgive sins but God alone?" (Mark 2:7).

Jesus knew what they were thinking and said to them, "Why are you thinking these things? Which is easier; to say to this paralyzed man, 'Your sins are forgiven,' or to say, 'Get up, take your mat and walk'? But I want you to know that the Son of Man has authority on earth to forgive sins." He then told the paralytic, "I tell you, get up, take your mat and go home" (Mark 2:8-11).

And so the paralytic was healed to the amazement of all who witnessed the miracle. Such is the faith we must have in Jesus as we follow Him. It is written that everyone who believes that Jesus is the Christ is born of God and that everyone born of God overcomes the world for "this is the victory that has overcome the world, even our faith" (1 John 5:1-4). Our faith in Christ will give us victory.

However, as human beings, our faith can be weak if we don't keep our eyes on Jesus. This was the case when Peter walked on water. Jesus had been praying alone on a mountainside. He had told His disciples to go ahead of Him in a boat. It was shortly before dawn.

When the boat was a good distance from the land, the disciples saw Jesus walking on water towards the boat. At first they were scared thinking that they were seeing a ghost. But Jesus told them: "Take courage! It is I. Don't be afraid" (Mathew 14:27).

Peter as usual became adventurous and asked the Lord if he could go to him. The Lord agreed and Peter walked on water as he went to Jesus. But when Peter saw the wind he became afraid and began to sink. He cried, "Lord save me!" (Mathew 14:30).

Then Jesus reached out and caught him telling him, "You of little faith, why did you doubt?" (Mathew 14:31). This is a lesson to us: We should keep our eyes focused on Jesus all the time and we should never be afraid.

12. Remember that you are paying the prize for others

Jesus paid the prize for us, yet He had no sin. He died to reclaim us and to reunite us with the Father and with Himself in the Kingdom of Heaven. And to say the truth, we did not deserve this mercy because we are a stiff-necked and stubborn people whose default mode is disobedience.

In the Footsteps of Jesus

It is by God's grace that we have been saved. And this is an unmerited favor. This step in carrying our own cross to follow Jesus is vital.

We must know that whatever we do is for the glory of the Lord and not for our own self gain. We have to accept that the burdens we carry may be for our children, brothers and sisters or for our community and are a cost that we must bear as we follow Jesus.

God has given us life and talents freely. So let us also give back freely to serve God and to care for His creation. As we carry the cross, let us not think of our own suffering but the suffering of others. Among the things we should do are the following:

- Do not judge others
- Do not accuse anyone because when you make people feel accused they will run away
- Be a true Christian: If you claim to be a Christian but live otherwise, you are using the name of the Lord in vain
- Love your enemies. Jesus said, "Love your enemies and pray for those who persecute you, that you may be sons of your Father in heaven. He causes his sun to rise on the evil and the good, and send rain on the righteous and the unrighteous." (Mathew 5:44-45)

- Freely you have received, freely give: Serve the poor, the widows and the orphans
- Always turn the other cheek. Leave vengeance to the Lord
- Pray for understanding so that we may hate the sins we commit
- Love sinners and pray for them

Let us not give in until we reach the crossing line. And when we get there, the reward will be assured in Christ Jesus. Let us remember the words of: "Now all has been heard; fear God and keep his commandments, for this is the whole duty of man" (Ecclesiastes 12:13). As we wait for the crossing line, let us do these three things:

- Fear God as our creator.
- Let us open our hearts for Christ to come in so that He causes us to be obedient.
- Let us fill our lamps with adequate oil as we await the second coming of the Lord.

"Do this in remembrance of me"

When the time came for Jesus to be arrested and tried, He gathered His disciples for the last supper. He sent Peter and John to make preparations for the Passover meal. So, at the last supper, He entered into a holy communion with them. First, Jesus washed the feet of His disciples and then

He gave them bread and a drink saying that He had eagerly awaited to share the meal with them before He suffered. As He broke the bread and gave it to them, He said, "This is my body, which is for you; do this in remembrance of me." Then he took the cup from which he gave them a drink saying to them, "This cup in the new covenant in my blood; do this, whenever you drink it, in remembrance of me" (1st Corinthians 11:24-25).

As we follow in the footsteps of Jesus, let us partake of the Holy Communion in remembrance of Him. The washing of feet is a symbol of humility and service to God. The breaking of the bread during the Holy Communion reminds us that Jesus is the bread of life that came from heaven to give us life eternal.

The bread is the word of God which we must eat every day to bring us closer to our Father. And the drink we partake of reminds us of the sacrifice Jesus made for us on the cross. This also reminds us that we must sacrifice and leave behind many good things as we follow our Lord.

Jesus gave us comforting words in the book of Mathew for He said, "All things have been committed to me by my father. No one knows the Son except the Father, and no one knows the Father except the Son and those to whom the Son chooses to reveal Him" (Mathew 11:27). And he added, "Come to me, all you who are weary and burdened, and I will give you rest. Take my yoke upon you and learn from me, for I am gentle and humble in heart, and you will find rest for your souls. For my yoke is easy and my burden is light" (Mathew 11:28-30).

Our Redeemer is gentle and humble. He is standing at the door. Let us open our hearts so that He can come in and cause us to follow Him faithfully. When He does, we will grow in spirit and will be more like Him in all we do. We will have the mark of Christ in us and anyone who sees us will see Jesus in us.

The Apostle Paul writes: "You are all sons of God through faith in Christ Jesus, for all of you who were baptized into Christ have clothed yourselves with Christ. There is neither a Jew nor Greek, slave nor free, male nor female, for you are all one in Christ Jesus" (Galatians 3:26-28).

In Christ Jesus, we are all one. Those who know Christ and are in Him must forget their race, tribe, clan or social class. When we fight in any institution or in any congregation to be led by those we consider as "our own" or who "look like us," we are essentially crucifying Christ yet again and we do not know Him.

It is important for those who follow in the footsteps of Christ to surrender and be in one body with Him. The Father made Jesus to be sin for us so that in Jesus we might become righteous and become a new creation. As it is written, "Therefore, if anyone is in Christ, he is a new creation, the old has gone, the new has come!" (2nd Corinthians 5:17).

Let us do an internal audit of ourselves and if we find any trace of tribalism or racism, we need prayers and we need to ask for forgiveness. The Lord Almighty is gracious. He will forgive us for He created us in His likeness and loves all His children equally. Christ is our example. Let us follow in His footsteps.

CHAPTER 11

JESUS IS COMING AGAIN

"Look, he is coming with the clouds" and "every eye will see him, even those who pierced him." Revelation 1:7

Jesus is coming again. This is the good news. We are certain of this because Jesus told us so. And, He is coming soon. For over two thousand years, we have been told that Jesus will return to take the elect home to inherit the Kingdom of Heaven.

But Jesus Himself declared that the end will not come until the gospel of the Kingdom of Heaven has been preached to the whole world as a testimony to all nations. He also said: "But about that day or the hour no one knows, not even the angels in heaven nor the Son, but only the Father" (Mathew 24:36).

Just like in the days of Noah, we have been warned and have been given enough notice. In the days of Noah, the Lord said: "I am going to put an end to all people, for the earth is filled with violence because of them. I am surely going to destroy both them and the earth" (Genesis 6:13). God gave the reason why He made this judgment: He had seen how great the wickedness of human beings had become and that "every inclination of the thoughts of the human heart was only evil all the time" (Genesis 6:5.) The

Jesus is Coming Again

Lord saw the corruption that had engulfed the world and the violence therein. He was disappointed by the disobedience of the human race and He declared, "I will wipe from the face of the earth the human race I have created – and with them the animals, the birds and the creatures that move along the ground – for I regret that I have made them" (Genesis 6:7).

But at the end of the floods when Noah, his wife and children and all the creatures that had survived came out of the Ark, the Lord said: "Never again will I curse the ground because of humans, even though every inclination of the human heart is evil from childhood. And never again will I destroy all living creatures, as I have done" (Genesis 8:21).

The plan of salvation that was there from the beginning, and was operationalized immediately after Adam and Eve disobeyed God, must have been hastened. Jesus was coming to rescue the elect. And He came in person to save the lost and to invite the elect to the Kingdom of Heaven. Whereas in Noah's days, people were given a relatively shorter notice, we have now been given over 2000 years to heed the call Jesus made to us saying: "Repent, for the Kingdom of Heaven is near" (Mathew 4:17). This redemption offer was made to all mankind. All that is required of us is to accept Jesus as our Lord and Savior and to repent all our sins. The rest we leave to Him because in the end, our salvation is by grace and grace alone.

The Testimony of Jesus

This is a call to all Christians: Wake up! For the coming of the Lord is near. Jesus simplified His messages to mankind. So let us not complicate God's message to the world especially now that the end is near. And the message is simple: **"Repent, for the Kingdom of Heaven is near."** This is all we need to preach. And if we have to add anything then all we need to say is, **"Jesus is coming again"**. Then we could add, "And He is coming soon." This would be enough.

Let us all wake up now lest we become like the five foolish virgins Jesus told us about. They were asleep while waiting for their bridegroom but with little oil in their lamps. When the time came and the bridegroom arrived, they had no oil in their lamps and could not find their way to meet him.

And again, to all Christians, let us wake up. Let us open our hearts and allow Christ to come in and open our eyes so that we can see that the time is up. The signs of the end of time are all around us.

Yes, let us pump in the oil so that we can be filled. To have this oil is to be filled with the Holy Spirit as we search for the Lord with all our hearts and with all our minds and we read His Word daily. Now is the time to do what the Lord said in the book of Deuteronomy when the He told the Children of Israel this: "These commandments I give you today are to be upon your hearts. Impress them on your

Jesus is Coming Again

children. Talk about them when you sit at home and when you walk along the road, when you lie down and when you get up. Tie them as symbols on your hands and bind them on your foreheads. Write them on the door-frames of your houses and on tour gates" (Deuteronomy 6:6-9).

Yes, this is the time to fill our hearts with the message of the Kingdom of Heaven instead of filling it with the desires of the world. It is time to go home to the Father and not to stay prosperous here on earth. Let us remember the words of Job after he had lost everything including all his children.

He said, "Naked I came from my mother's womb, and naked I shall depart. The Lord gave and the Lord has taken away; may the name of the Lord be praised" (Job 1:21). Jesus also said, "What good will it be for someone to gain the whole world, yet forfeit his soul? Or what can anyone give in exchange for their soul?" (Mathew 16:26). So let us stop craving for good life here on earth and start craving for the Kingdom of Heaven.

Our Father is good, He will take care of us according to His purpose for us. He provides for the wicked as well as for the righteous. He provides for the birds in the air and the animals in the wilderness and He will provide for us. In any case, it is time for all of us to be content with whatever we have as we begin to earnestly seek the Kingdom of Heaven with all our hearts and with all our minds. I want all of us to say this together: "Let us repent for the Kingdom of Heaven is near." This simple message from Christ must ring in our ears all the time. And, we must spread it to the ends of the world.

We must spread the good news that Jesus is coming again to take us home where we will be with Him and the Father in the Kingdom of Heaven forever. Now, I want to come back to the question we have already addressed in earlier chapters.

And this is: **"With all this evidence and the Testimony of Jesus, what are we waiting for?"** And let me add one more questions to all of us, "For how long shall we continue to harden our hearts and refuse to accept Jesus as our Lord and Savior and to surrender to Him?

The end is very near

Jesus said in a parable, **"Look at the fig tree and all the trees. When they sprout leaves, you can see for yourselves and know that summer is near.** Even so, when you see these things happen, you know that the Kingdom of God is near" (Luke 21:29-31).

Jesus was talking to His disciples about the end time. He said to them that a time was coming when not one stone will be left on another at the time of the end. "Teacher," they asked Him, "When will these things happen? And what will be the sign that they are about to take place?" (Luke 21:5-7). In His answer, Jesus listed a number of things including the following as outlined in the book of Luke chapter 21 verses 8 to 27:

- Many will come in His name claiming to be Him.
- People will hear of wars and uprisings.
- Nation will rise against nation and kingdom against kingdom.
- There will be great earthquakes, famines and pestilence in various places.
- Followers of Christ will be persecuted. "They will hand you over to synagogues and put you in prison, and you will be brought before kings and governors, all on account of my name," He said.
- You will be betrayed even by parents, brothers and sisters, relatives and friends, and they will put some of you to death.
- Everyone will hate you because of me.
- There will be signs in the sun, moon and stars.
- On the earth, nations will be in anguish and perplexity at the roaring and tossing of the sea (remember the Tsunami in Thailand).
- People will faint from terror, apprehensive of what is coming on the world, for heavenly bodies will be shaken.

The Testimony of Jesus

Jesus said, "When these things begin to take place, stand and lift up your heads, because your redemption is drawing near" (Luke 21:28). As we ponder over Jesus' message of what will happen as the end of time gets near, let us take a look at what is happening today in many parts of the world:

1. We are making it difficult for God to contend with us any more

In the days of Noah, it is written that "The sons of God saw that the daughters of humans were beautiful, and they married any of them they chose." The Lord said, "My Spirit will not contend with humans forever, for they are mortal; their days will be a hundred and twenty years" (Genesis 6:2-3).

Until then, people lived much longer. For example, it was not until after Noah became 500 years old that he became the father of Shem, Ham and Japheth (Genesis 5:32).

But the Lord cut short the years people would live as He could not contend with human beings anymore. The story did not end with immorality of mankind as the "earth was corrupt in God's sight and was full of violence. God saw how corrupt the earth had become, for all the people on the earth had corrupted their ways" (Genesis 6:11-12).

This sounds very much like the times we are living in today. It is not difficult for us to see how corrupt people have become all over the world. The reasons that led to the floods during Noah's time are here today. In fact, they are worse.

Let us consider the following:

- Sexual immorality is perhaps worse now than it has ever been. The so called sexual revolution of the sixties and seventies liberalized sexual relations and contributed to growing sexual immorality. The Apostle Paul wrote about sexual immorality and just how much it hurts the Lord when one gets involved in it. Paul wrote: "Flee from sexual immorality. **All other sins a person commits are outside the body, but whoever sins sexually, sins against their own body.** Do you not know that your bodies are temples of the Holy Spirit, who is in you, whom you have received from God? You are not your own; you were bought at a price. Therefore honor God with your bodies" (1st Corinthians 6:18-20).
- The family unit is being destroyed. Divorce has become a common occurrence and marriage no longer means what God intended it be - a holy union between a man and a woman.
- The worst form of sexual disobedience by man is the ordination of homosexual priests to preach the word of God from the pulpit. I do not condemn homosexuals because we are all sinners. But, I do not understand why

churches can be so disobedient to God to the extent that they can go ahead with ordination of priests in a manner that is contrary to Biblical principles.

- It is also easy to see that the world is now lost in worshipping other gods. New gods have now emerged. I consider anything that takes full attention and commitment from a person, away from the Lord Almighty, to be his or her god. For example, all over the world, people have turned to materialism and are idolizing many things including sports. We have seen people committing suicide simply because their teams have not performed to their expectations. I know people who lose their appetite and would not eat just because their football teams lost a game. They live for these teams and have become prisoners to the games they watch week in week out. Such people have little or no time to search for the Lord Almighty. I must confess that I had also been caught up in this confusion. I have prayed and prayed for the Lord to free me from this. And I thank Him for his grace and kindness towards me in this regard.
- For many of us, our cars, houses and the money we seek have taken centre stage in our lives leaving us little or no time for God.
- The secular world is growing more and more influential in our lives especially among the young people who are

lost in their cell phones, internet, television, movies and music. They have centered their lives on individualism believing that they can do all things through their own effort. They do not give any room for God in their lives.

- One of the reasons that led to the floods in the time of Noah was the corruption and the violence in the world. It is written: "Now the earth was corrupt in God's sight and was full of violence. God saw how corrupt the earth had become, for all the people on earth had corrupted their ways" (Genesis 6:11-12). Well, well, well. How about us today? Are we any different? Corruption in many parts of the world has reached a boiling point. Just take a look at the misrule by various leaders in the world including the Middle East and my continent of Africa that is leading to severe suffering of God's children. These corrupt governments and leaders are certainly making God unhappy and the Lord may soon decide that "enough is enough".

- As we have seen above, Jesus said many things that will happen at the end of time. One of the signs he talked about is that people will faint from terror, apprehensive of what is coming. Well, we know just how much the world today has been engulfed in terror making people afraid and insecure.

2. **The assurance Christ gave that the end will come only after the message of the Kingdom is preached to the ends of the world in now being fulfilled.**

Jesus told us that the time and the hour of His second coming are only known to the Father. He said: "But about that day or hour no one knows, not even the angels in heaven, nor the Son, but only the Father.

As it was in the days of Noah, so it will be at the coming of the Son of Man. For in the days before the flood, people were eating and drinking, marrying and giving in marriage, up to the day Noah entered the ark, and they knew nothing about what would happen until the flood came and took them all away. That is how it will be at the coming of the Son of Man" (Mathew 24:36-39).

But Jesus also went ahead to tell us to watch out for the signs of His return. And the one cardinal sign Jesus gave us is this: "And this gospel of the kingdom will be preached in the whole world as a testimony to all nations, and then the end will come" (Mathew 24:14).

I want to imagine that because Jesus does not want anyone to be lost, it was very critical for Him to ensure that everyone on the face of the earth had a chance to hear and receive the message of the Kingdom of Heaven. He certainly knew that a time would come when this would be possible. Well, that time is here now. I want to also imagine that Jesus must have known that as knowledge increased, a day would come when it would be possible to reach the entire world in the shortest time possible. With the invention of the internet and the social networks which have the potential of reaching hundreds of millions of people in real time, this day has arrived.

Today, it is possible for the gospel of the Kingdom of Heaven to be preached to the whole world. The key words here are "to be preached in the whole world." I do believe that it is not about converting the whole world to Christianity. It is about giving the whole world a chance to choose.

There are those who will choose to find the gospel of the Kingdom of Heaven and then there are those who will rebel. The important thing is that the gospel is preached to the whole world and that everyone has a chance to hear it. Let me ask this: **Now, with the internet and the social media, the worldwide television and the radios, can anyone doubt that today the gospel cannot be preached to the whole world? If the answer is no, then let us get ready.** Jesus is coming again. And He is coming soon. Let us be watchful as we await His return.

3. Knowledge will increase

The Lord said this to Daniel who experienced many visions regarding the end of time: "But you Daniel, shut up the words, and seal the book until the time of the end; many shall run to and fro, and knowledge shall increase."

The Testimony of Jesus

(Daniel 12:4, NKJV) Yes, many will go here and there. Cars and airplanes were not invented then. But they must have been part of the vision the Lord gave to Daniel. They are the product of increased knowledge and they have made it possible for people to travel everywhere, going here and there. One cannot imagine what it will be like if this level of knowledge expansion can continue for say another one hundred years.

Will we have flying cars which by design cannot collide against each other in the air? Or will we have robots doing all the office work while the rest of us work from home? And will scientists continue to do their experiments on God's created nature, altering genetic materials at will, to the displeasure of the Lord? Can the rivers, the lakes and the air we breathe contain the pollution by the products of increased knowledge? I do not know for how long this expansion of knowledge can continue. But it is clear that we are reaching the limit and what will be left is for the Lord to come and take us home.

4. Self-declared prophets

Today, the world has seen the emergence of self-declared false prophets who are deceiving their followers by preaching prosperity in the name of Jesus and are deliberately ignoring to focus on the gospel of the Kingdom of Heaven. They are ignoring the fact that a life filled with Jesus is an abundant life. In addition to preaching prosperity, they have brought entertainment and dance to God's house.

Let me not judge anyone for the final judge is Christ. However, the last message of Jesus before His ascension was: "Therefore go and make disciples of all nations, baptizing them in the name of the Father and of the Son and of the Holy Spirit, teaching them to obey everything I have commanded you. And surely I am with you always, to the very end of the age" (Mathew 28:19-20).

This is the Great Commission which we should all focus on. But instead, many have chosen to focus is on earthly things. This prosperity message is also making it impossible for people to hear the message of the Kingdom of Heaven. I urge the prosperity preachers to change and start preparing people for the Kingdom of Heaven because Jesus said that this message of the kingdom must be preached to the whole world before He comes.

5. Places of worship defiled

In many countries today, places of worship have become social clubs, gossip houses and entertainment centers. Even sectionalism and tribalism have become prominent in many churches today. People want to identify with "their own" instead of embracing all children of God equally. Well, one thing we can be sure of is that when Jesus returns, the words race and tribe will be wiped out of the heavenly dictionary. Your race and tribe will be irrelevant. We will all belong to one race called Children of God. Further, today it is not about selling sacrificial animals and birds in the temples as was the case when Jesus overturned tables and drove out the cattle, sheep and doves which were being sold. He also scattered coins belonging to money changers.

Jesus said to those who were selling in the temple, "Get these things out of here! How dare you turn my Father's house into a market!" (John 2:16). Today, one may as well ask: "How can we turn God's houses into social clubs, dance halls, gossip places and money-making centres?" The above are only but a few of what we see happening around us. I believe that there is much more that can be written. So let us just keep watch and focus on Christ as we await the second coming.

The dead will rise

The dead are dead and will rise at the second coming of our Lord. Even Daniel was told, "As for you, go away till the end. You will rest, and then at the end of the days you will rise to receive your allotted inheritance" (Daniel 12:13).

Yes, the dead are asleep and are in their graves awaiting the sound of trumpet at the second coming of Christ. Jesus said: "Very truly I tell you, a time is coming and has now come when the dead will hear the voice of the Son of God and those who hear will live" (John 5:25). He added, "Do not be amazed at this, for a time is coming when all who are in their graves will hear his voice and come out – those who have done what is good will rise to live, and those who have done what is evil will rise to be condemned" (John 5:28-29). Jesus was obviously talking about His second coming.

In the book of Ecclesiastes, it is written: "For the living know that they will die, but the dead know nothing" (Ecclesiastes 9:5). Yes, the dead are in the ground and we should not be deceived that when people die they go straight to heaven. When we die, and the breath of life is taken from us, we remain right here on earth waiting for second coming of the Lord.

The Apostle Paul wrote: "So will it be with the resurrection of the dead. The body that is sown is perishable, it is raised imperishable, it is sown in dishonor, it is raised in glory, it is sown in weakness, it is raised in power, it is sown a natural body, it is raised a spiritual body" (1st Corinthians 15:42-44). He added, "Listen, I tell you a mystery: We will not all sleep, but we will all be changed, in a flash, in the twinkling of an eye, at the last trumpet. For the trumpet will sound, the dead will be raised imperishable, and we will be changed" (1st Corinthians 15:51-52).

It is also written: "For the Lord himself will come down from heaven, with a loud command, with the voice of the archangel and with the trumpet call of God, and the dead in Christ will rise first. After that, we who are still alive and are left will be caught up together with them in the clouds to meet the Lord in the air. And so we will be with the Lord forever" (1st Thessalonians 4:13-17). The time and day of the coming of the Lord is certainly not known. What is known is that the "day of the Lord will come like a thief in the night" (1st Thessalonians 5:2).

Jesus is coming in a person's lifetime plus one second

As it has already been stated, we must prepare ourselves for the second coming of Jesus for the hour is near. And I want to imagine that for many of us, the coming is very near indeed because Jesus will come in our lifetime plus one second.

This is because at the hour and the second we breathe our last breath, our clock in this earth stops. We die and go to sleep. And when the trumpet will sound at the second coming of Jesus, we shall rise in a "twinkling of an eye" as Jesus descends down with His angels. We shall arise from our graves from the deep sleep during which we knew nothing.

At the sound of the trumpet and in a twinkling of an eye or in a second, we will wake up. And this is why it is important to realize that Jesus will come in one's lifetime plus one second because when we die, our clock only starts again at our resurrection. Let me emphasis this again: When we die, we go to asleep and the next time we wake up we will see Christ coming down in His glory. So for every individual the time to prepare for the Kingdom of Heaven is now.

He will separate the sheep from the goats

When Jesus comes, all the nations will be gathered before Him and He will separate the people one from another as a shepherd separates the sheep from the goats. He will put the sheep on His right and the goats on His left. Jesus added: "Then the King will say to those on His right, "Come you who are blessed by my Father; take your inheritance, the kingdom prepared for you since the creation of the world. For I was hungry and you gave me something to eat, I was thirsty and you gave me something to drink, I was a stranger and you invited me in, I needed clothes and you clothed me, I was sick and you looked after me, I was in prison and you came to visit me" Mathew 25: 34-36).

Jesus said, "Then the righteous will answer him 'Lord, when did we see you hungry and feed you, or thirsty and give you something to drink? When did we see you a stranger and invite you in, or needing clothes and clothe you? When did we see you sick or in prison and go to visit you?'" (Mathew 25: 37-39). In verse 40, Jesus says: "The King will reply, 'Truly I tell you, whatever you did for one of the least of these brothers and sisters of mine, you did for me.'"

For those on the left of the Lord who did none of the above, the Lord will say: "Depart from me, you who are cursed, into the eternal fire prepared for the devil and his angels" (Mathew 24:41).

It is obvious that we should not try to bribe our way into heaven by intentionally doing good works so as to gain God's favor, hoping to be seated on His right side where the sheep are gathered. Instead, we must seek first the Kingdom of God and His righteousness so that Christ may dwell in our hearts and cause us to do good without even knowing.

It is written that the elect are those who are obedient to God and have kept His commandments by His Grace, and they are those who hold on to the testimony of Jesus (Revelation 12:17). For when we have Christ in us, doing good, especially for those who are needy, will be inevitable.

Hope in the second coming

Jesus is coming again. And He is coming soon. This is the message we must spread to the ends of the world. And this is the good news that brings hope to all who love the Lord. We are waiting for the Return in the assurance of our salvation because of the Love of God. Through His grace we are saved. We have the justification that has been bestowed upon us through the sacrificial death of Jesus on the cross. Justification, which is the removal of all our sins

Jesus is Coming Again

and guilt and the declaration that we are "Not Guilty", is the righteousness of Jesus which has been accredited to sinners, making the sinners to also become righteous. This is not earned. It is unmerited favor through God's grace. Jesus has redeemed us and by His stripes we have the privilege of being united once again with the Father.

The Apostle Paul writes: "For all have sinned and fall short of the glory of God, and are justified freely by his grace through the redemption that came by Christ Jesus" (Romans 3:23-24). He adds, "God made him who had no sin to be sin for us, so that in him we might become the righteousness of God" (2nd Corinthians 5:21). This, indeed, is the good news. All that is now required of us is to accept Jesus as our Lord and Savior and then leave the rest to the Lord.

Further, it is important for Christians to grow in the knowledge of Christ. We who have been created in God's image should follow in the footstep of Jesus and aim for intimate relationships with Him. It is written: "In your hearts set apart Christ as Lord.

Always be prepared to give an answer to everyone who asks you to give the reason for the hope that you have. But do this with gentleness and respect, keeping a clear conscience so that those who speak maliciously against your good behavior in Christ may be ashamed of their slander" (1st Peter 3:15-16). Yes, let us be set apart for Christ.

The Testimony of Jesus

Through the work of the Holy Spirit, we will receive sanctification which is a process of steady growth in Christ. Sanctification is to be set apart for Christ and be more like Him. The Holy Spirit will work in us so that we will be dead to sin and experience the presence of God in our lives. The Apostle Paul says, "For you died, and your life is now hidden with Christ in God" (Colossians 3:3).

By the grace of God, we will hate sin and be cleansed daily as we become more and more like Jesus. As it is written, "For the grace of God has appeared that offers salvation to all people. It teaches us to say 'NO' to ungodliness and worldly passions, and to live self-controlled, upright and godly lives in this present age, while we wait for the blessed hope – the appearing of the glory of our God and savior, Jesus Christ" (Titus 2:11-13).

As we await the second coming, we must spend more time with God, digging deeper into the word of God. We must ruminate upon scriptures all the time so that they can become part of our system. In doing so, we will draw nearer to God and He will fill our hearts with joy.

And yes, we must pray and be willing to open the door of our heart for Christ to come in and eat with us so that we can live life abundantly.

We who have been justified by the cross and set apart by the work of the Holy Spirit have hope in the second coming. As we experience all this, let us give thanks to the

Lord Almighty. Let us sing songs of praise unto Him. And let us always remember that the elect are those who obey the Lord, keeping all His commandments, and those who hold to the testimony of Jesus.

A new heaven and new earth

How will it be in the end when we meet the Alpha and the Omega? One chapter will have been closed and a new chapter will begin.

The fallen world will be no more and the deceiver will also be no more. A new world will be created for the elect to inherit the Kingdom of Heaven and the Lord will live among them.

The prophet Isaiah writes about this new earth in Isaiah chapter 65:

Vs 17: "Behold, I will create new heavens and a new earth (says the Sovereign Lord). The former things will not be remembered, nor will they come to mind."

Vs 18: "But be glad and rejoice forever in what I will create, for I will create Jerusalem to be a delight and its people a joy."

Vs 19: "I will rejoice over Jerusalem and delight in my people; the sound of weeping and crying will be heard in it no more."

Vs 22: "No longer will they build houses and others live in them or plant and other eat. For as the days of a tree, so will be the days of my people; my chosen ones will long enjoy the works of their hands."

Vs 24: "Before they call I will answer; while they are still speaking I will hear."

Vs 25: "The wolf and the lamb will feed together, and the lion will eat straw like the ox, but dust will be serpent's food. They will neither harm nor destroy on all my holy mountain."

Similarly, John the Revelator saw a new heaven and a new earth in his vision. He writes: "Then I saw a new heaven and a new earth, for the first heaven and the first earth had passed away, and there was no longer any sea. I saw the Holy City, the New Jerusalem, coming down out of heaven from God, prepared as a bride beautifully dressed for her husband.

And I heard a loud voice from the throne saying, "Now the dwelling of God is with men, and he will live with them. They will be His people, and God Himself will be with them and be their God" (Revelation 21:1-3).

In this kingdom, there will be no more death and no more sin. It is written that, "No eye has seen, no ear has heard, no mind has conceived what God has prepared for those who love Him" (1st Corinthians 2:9). It is not possible for us to imagine just how wonderful the new earth that awaits the elect will be.

How I long to see Jesus when He returns! The Lord our God will surely live and dwell among us and reign forever and ever. When he comes, all will see Him for it is written, "For as lightning that comes from the east is visible even in the west, so will be the coming of the Son of Man" (Mathew 24:27).

We are called upon to have faith and wait because, "In just a little while; he who is coming will come and will not delay" (Hebrew 10:37). Yes, Jesus is coming again. Jesus says: "It is done. I am the Alpha and the Omega, the Beginning and the End. To him who is thirsty I will give to drink without cost from the spring of the water of life. He who overcomes will inherit all this and I will be his God and he will be my son" (Revelation 21:6-7).

And he adds, "Behold, I am coming soon! My reward is with me, and I will give to everyone according to what he has done" (Revelation 22:12).

Finally, in concluding this book, let us consider these recurring questions once more: **"With all this evidence and the Testimony of Jesus, what are we waiting for?** For how long shall we continue to harden our hearts and refuse to accept Jesus as our Lord and Savior and to surrender to Him? And, are we willing to open that door so that Christ can come in and eat with us?

And there are two more questions we Christians need to ask ourselves in each and every situation and whenever we are doing anything or intend to do anything: 1) What would Christ want me to do? And 2) Am I giving glory to the Almighty God in whatever I am doing or in everything I am planning to do?

May the Lord Almighty bless us all as we come face to face with the Testimony of Jesus and as we await His second coming.

Amen.

EPILOGUE

We have been called upon to testify that Jesus Christ is our Lord and Savior. He died for us on the cross and atoned for all our sins. By so doing, Jesus made it possible for the lost children of God to be reunited with the Father.

This book on the Testimony of Jesus has highlighted who Jesus is and how He is coming again to take us home. We have seen that we need to drink from the Spring of Living Water and to carry our cross and follow Jesus.

We have encountered the message of the Kingdom of Heaven and have been called upon to repent for the Kingdom is near.

We have witnessed the oneness of the Father, the Son and the Holy Spirit for they are one in the Triune God. Jesus said, "Whoever hates me hates my Father as well" (John 15:23).

By loving Jesus, we love the Father and when we love the Father we also love Jesus whom He sent to save us. Our duty now is to respond and ask the Lord to soften our stubborn hearts. It is our duty as created beings to fear God and give Him glory for it is written, "Now all has been heard; here is the conclusion of the matter: Fear God and keep his commandments, for this is the whole duty of man" (Ecclesiastes 12:13). Our entire system has been wired for worship. If we are not watchful, we will find ourselves worshipping anything. Today, people are worshipping idols, wealth, sports and many other gods. But as the salt of the earth, we can step out and be different as we spread the good news of the Kingdom of Heaven. We can be bold as we share the testimony with others. Jesus said, "You are the salt of the earth. But if the salt loses its saltiness, how can it be made salty again? It is no longer good for anything, except to be thrown out and tramped by men" (Mathew 5:13).

We are in danger of losing our saltiness if we just sit back and wait for others to do God's work, especially at this time that we are so near to the end. Jesus also told us, "You are the light of the world. A city on a hill cannot be hidden. Neither do people light a lamp and put it under a bowl! Instead they put it on its stand and it gives light to everyone in the house. In the same way, let your light shine before men, that they may see your good deeds and praise your Father in heaven" (Mathew 5:14-16).

In all this, we are reminded that the "Lord is good and he is our refuge in times of trouble and he cares for those who trust in him" Nahum 1:7. Let us trust in the Lord. His promises never fail. All we need to do is to open the doors of our hearts so that Christ can come in and eat with us and cause us to follow in His footsteps. The Lord has shown us what is good and requires us to "act justly, and to love mercy and to walk humbly" with Him (Micah 6:8).

Epilogue

As we ruminate upon the Word of God, we need to examine ourselves and do **a Christian Self Audit**. In doing this, we need to seek the Holy Spirit to guide us as we face various issues in our lives. We need to be careful not to condemn ourselves for we are born sinners. All we need to do is to love God and hate sin. Among the questions and issues we need to ask of ourselves are the following:

- When faced with any situation, we need to ask ourselves these questions: what would Jesus say? What would Jesus do?
- In everything I do, am I giving glory to God?
- Do I really know Jesus? For to know Him is to do His will and to follow in His footsteps.
- Am I a judge of others, forming opinion on things I may not understand?
- How have I shown compassion to those in need? Or, are they a burden to me? Do I do good things to be seen by others or do I do them because of the love of God in me?
- Do I love my neighbor or do I love only those who look like me: My clan, my tribe and those in my social class? Do I hate people just because they do not look like me? Is there any trace of racism or tribalism in me? Remember the words of Jesus when He said this: "They hated me without a reason" John 15:25. If you hate someone just

because of their tribe or race, you hate them without a reason.
- Do I know that I am a sinner?
- Do I love my enemies and pray for them?
- Do I forgive others as I would want the Lord to forgive me?
- Do I really love God? Do I read God's Word daily and seek to know Him with all my heart and with my entire mind? Have I created enough time to be with my God in prayer and in meditation upon His Word? The Lord says that to love Him is to keep His Commandments: How am I doing with regard to this?
- What is the level of self-discipline in me? Am I trustworthy? Do I have integrity?
- Am I involved in corruption and corrupt practices?
- Am I lustful and am I covetous?
- Am I fighting for power or glory even in God's church or do I wait to be an elect, chosen by God?
- Do I hate sin? Am I being obedient unto the Lord keeping all His Commandments including keeping His Sabbath?

The above are only but a sample of things in our lives over which we may have little or no control. We need to pray and ask God to forgive us for we have all sinned and fallen short of His glory. We must accept that it is only by

Epilogue

His grace that we can grow daily to overcome temptations such as the ones stated above.

The good news is that we are a blessed people because of the blood of Jesus and because we have the Holy Spirit who ministers to us–we who are made in the likeness of God–so that we can become like Him. We are strengthened daily by God's Word for it is written: "I have hidden your word in my heart that I might not sin against you" (Psalm 119:11). We need to have strong faith for it is written that the righteous will live by faith (Romans 1:17; Habakkuk 2:4).

Let us pray that our faith will grow day by day as we await the Second Coming. And let us have hope that on that day when the trumpet will sound and the Lord shall descend, we will rise and join Him in celebrating the final victory.

Finally, let us give thanks to the Father for the blood of the Lamb that has redeemed us all. And let us pray this prayer:

> Our gracious and loving Father, the Lord God of the Universe; you are the Almighty, the God of Abraham, Isaac and Jacob. You are our Creator and we are the created. Praise and honor and glory be unto thee. You are Holy and Worthy to be praised. You are the omnipotent, omniscient, and

omnipresent God. We thank you Father for your Love and for your Grace. We thank you for the love of Jesus our Lord and Savior who has redeemed us: He is the one with whom you created the Universe. We thank you for the love of the Holy Spirit, our Counselor. May your name be praised for ever and ever.

Father, in the name of Jesus, help us to surrender daily to your will, Oh God. And turn our hardened hearts unto thee. Open our hearts so that Christ our Savior and our Redeemer can come in and dwell in us, and cause us to be obedient unto thee. And open our eyes so that we may see. Lord keep us from the evil one as we journey in this sinful world. Our Father, forgive us for we have all sinned against you.

And may we worship thee and thee alone.

We come to you in this prayer in the precious name of Jesus Christ our Lord and Savior as we stay in hope and await His second coming.

Amen!

www.ingramcontent.com/pod-product-compliance
Lightning Source LLC
Chambersburg PA
CBHW060502090426
42735CB00011B/2076